GETTING THROUGH THE

TOUGH STUFF

WORKBOOK

GETTING THROUGH THE

TOUGH STUFF

WORKBOOK

It's Always Something!

C~HARLES~ R. S~WINDOLL~

W P~UBLISHING~ G~ROUP~
A Division of Thomas Nelson Publishers
Since 1798

www.wpublishinggroup.com

GETTING THROUGH THE TOUGH STUFF WORKBOOK

Charles R. Swindoll

Published by Nelson Reference and Electronics, a division of Thomas Nelson, Inc., P. O. Box 141000, Nashville, Tennessee, 37214.

Nelson Reference and Electronics books may be purchased in bulk for educational, business, fundraising, or sales promotional use. For information, please email SpecialMarkets@ThomasNelson.com.

Getting Through the Tough Stuff was created from the audio series *Christ at the Crossroads* for which a study guide was previously published by Insight for Living: Copyright © 1991 by Charles R. Swindoll. Revised edition: Copyright © 1998 by Charles R. Swindoll.

Original outlines, charts, and transcripts: Copyright ℗ © 1990 by Charles R. Swindoll.

Unless otherwise identified, Scripture references used in this book are from the *New American Standard Bible* (NASB). Copyright © 1960, 1962, 1963, 1968, 1971, 1972, 1973, 1975, 1977, 1995 by The Lockman Foundation. Used by permission. All rights reserved. (www.lockman.org).

Scriptures identified as MSG are taken from *The Message,* copyright © 1993, 1994, 1995, 1996, 2000, 2001, 2002 by NavPress Publishing Group. Used by permission. All rights reserved.

An effort has been made to locate sources and obtain permission where necessary for the quotations used in this book. In the event of any unintentional omission, a modification will gladly be incorporated in future printings.

Library of Congress Cataloging-in-Publication Data

ISBN 0-8499-4469-4

Printed in the United States of America
05 06 07 08 VG 5 4 3 2

Getting Through the Tough Stuff Workbook

Charles R. Swindoll has devoted his life to the clear, practical teaching and application of God's Word and His amazing grace. A pastor at heart, Chuck has served as senior pastor to congregations in Texas, Massachusetts, and California. He currently pastors Stonebriar Community Church in Frisco, Texas, but Chuck's listening audience extends far beyond a local church body. As a leading program in Christian broadcasting, *Insight for Living* airs in major Christian radio markets around the world, reaching churched and unchurched people groups in languages they can understand. Chuck's extensive writing ministry has also served the body of Christ worldwide, and his leadership as president and now chancellor of Dallas Theological Seminary has helped prepare and equip a new generation for ministry. Chuck and Cynthia, his partner in life and ministry, have four grown children and ten grandchildren.

Based on the original outlines, charts, and transcripts of Charles R. Swindoll's sermons, the workbook text was written by Marla Alupoaicei, Th.M., Dallas Theological Seminary. Contextual support material was provided by the Creative Ministries Department of Insight for Living.

Editor in Chief: Cynthia Swindoll
Director: Mark Gaither
Editors: Kathryn Moore, Greg Smith, Amy Snedaker
Research Assistant: Michael Kibbe

A Letter from Chuck Swindoll

Olympic athletes know what it takes to earn the gold medal. *Discipline. Sacrifice. Ambition. Drive. Hard work. Repetition. Strength training. A proper diet.* All athletes train tirelessly to reach a single goal—the opportunity to stand on the center platform with gleaming gold medallions around their necks, tears of emotion welling up in their eyes as their country's national anthem soars through the rafters of the packed stadium.

As each competitor stands on the platform, overcome with the emotions of victory, another person stands in the shadows, filled with joy and pride—a coach. No Olympic athlete makes it to that platform without a seasoned coach who has taught his or her protégé all the ins and outs of the sport.

We have the most outstanding coach ever—Jesus. He's the only One who fully understands how tough it is to leap all the painful hurdles that life presents. Christ has already completed the race of life, winning an incredible victory over death and the grave in order to offer us new life. Jesus knows how we must run so that when we stand before Him in glory, we may enjoy rewards that only eternity can measure.

Our coach calls us to a life of not merely surviving, but thriving. He calls us to overcome evil and to live an abundant, victorious life. He promises to abide in us, and He calls us to abide in Him. In order to do so, we must tackle our trials using the most powerful weapon available—the Word of God, described in Ephesians 6:17 as "the sword of the Spirit."

In this workbook, you'll learn more about fourteen of the most difficult hurdles that believers must leap. You'll answer specific questions that will help you evaluate your spiritual life, pinpoint your particular strengths, and address your weaknesses at this stage of your journey. Most importantly, you'll learn how to apply the principles of God's Word to the tough stuff you face each day of your own life.

So join us on our journey toward the finish line. You'll discover how to stay focused on the goal as you press on despite setbacks and roadblocks. You'll learn how to establish a rock-solid, disciplined faith that will help you to compete well, even when times get tough. So lace up your running shoes and fix your eyes on the prize. There's a race to be run.

Let's go!

—Charles R. Swindoll

Contents

A Letter from Chuck Swindoll   vii

How To Use This Workbook   xi

Chapter 1   1
Getting Through the Tough Stuff of Temptation

Chapter 2   13
Getting Through the Tough Stuff of Misunderstanding

Chapter 3   27
Getting Through the Tough Stuff of Anxiety

Chapter 4   39
Getting Through the Tough Stuff of Shame

Chapter 5   53
Getting Through the Tough Stuff of Doubt

Chapter 6   67
Getting Through the Tough Stuff of Divorce

Chapter 7   81
Getting Through the Tough Stuff of Remarriage

Chapter 8   95
Getting Through the Tough Stuff of Confrontation

Chapter 9   III
Getting Through the Tough Stuff of Pain

Chapter 10   125
Getting Through the Tough Stuff of Prejudice

Chapter II   139
Getting Through the Tough Stuff of Hypocrisy

Chapter 12   153
Getting Through the Tough Stuff of Inadequacy

Chapter 13   167
Getting Through the Tough Stuff of Disqualification

Chapter 14   181
Getting Through the Tough Stuff of Death

Notes   195

Books for Probing Further   203

HOW TO USE THIS WORKBOOK

The goal of this workbook is simple: to provide you with encouragement, biblical principles, application, and practical insights that will help you get through the tough stuff that life sends your way. This workbook serves as an ideal tool for personal devotions, small-group studies, and church curriculum.

Personal Devotions—When your one-on-one time with God needs direction, this interactive workbook guides you on the path toward greater wisdom, knowledge, and spiritual maturity.

Small-Group Bible Studies—When your small group desires to lay biblical foundations and build authentic community, this study guide provides you with a blueprint for learning God's Word and encouraging each other as you live together under His construction.

Church Curriculum—When your church body needs a resource that offers real answers to tough questions, this workbook provides biblical truth, straight answers, and life-application questions in an exciting, conversation-stimulating format.

You'll find two special features in each chapter of this workbook. These features will help you further unpack the intricacies of Scripture and cultivate deeper intimacy with the Almighty.

GETTING TO THE ROOT

In this section, you'll learn the origins and meanings of Hebrew and Greek words from the original biblical text. You'll discover how to better understand and apply specific scriptural terms.

TAKING TRUTH TO HEART

In this section, you'll have the opportunity for personal reflection and deeper soul-searching. You'll interact with principles from God's Word and the workbook chapter and integrate them into your life.

Our prayer is that the biblical principles and applications you glean from this workbook will revolutionize your spiritual life. As you incorporate what you've learned and seek God more deeply, you'll gain the faith and courage to face the tough stuff of life with confidence.

one

GETTING THROUGH THE
TOUGH STUFF OF TEMPTATION

The gospel accounts of Jesus's betrayal and crucifixion graphically illustrate that if *anyone* faced the tough stuff of life, it was Christ. The depth of Jesus's suffering truly defies description. But the greater question that arises in the face of such suffering is *why?* Why did Jesus have to endure so much pain?

That's just it—He didn't *have* to; He *chose* to. He willingly endured the torture of the cross in order to fully relate to us in our humanity, redeem us from our sinfulness, and reconcile us to God so we could enjoy a close relationship with our heavenly Father.

Because God's Son experienced the same ups and downs of life on earth that we have, we can trust that He knows our needs. His short life was marked by trials, but He never succumbed to temptation. At each pressure point, instead of letting sin enter His life, He turned to His Father for strength to pass every one of life's tests.

In this workbook, you'll discover practical ways that you, too, can get through the tough stuff of life without buckling under the strain of your trials. As you begin to integrate the principles of God's living Word into your life, you'll begin to experience the spiritual renewal, growth, and encouragement that you've been longing for.

Jesus's Encounter with the Tempter

About the time Jesus turned thirty, He hugged His family good-bye and left home forever, heading for the Jordan River region in Judea. His cousin John the Baptist baptized Him there, and God announced, "This is My beloved Son, in whom I am well-pleased" (Matthew 3:17). After Jesus's baptism, the Spirit led Him into

GETTING TO THE ROOT

The Greek word *peirazo* used in Matthew 4:1 may be translated "to test" or "to tempt." This term refers to the positive development of an individual's character through testing, as well as to the exposure of a person to certain temptations to see how he or she will respond.[1]

the wilderness "to be tempted by the devil" (4:1).

The drab desert stretched for miles in every direction, devoid of any sign of life. There in the wilderness, Satan bombarded the Savior with three of the toughest temptations imaginable. The devil had custom designed each of these temptations to lure Jesus away from His mission. On God's calendar, this period of time must have stood out in history, the days marked with big red Xs as some of the most difficult in Jesus's life.

Three Tests

A Personal Test

The first test was of a personal nature. Drawing upon what the Father had called Jesus at His baptism—"My beloved Son"—Satan dared Christ to prove His identity with a dazzling display of power.

> Then Jesus was led up by the Spirit into the wilderness to be tempted by the devil. And after He had fasted forty days and forty nights, He then became hungry. And the tempter came and said to Him, "If You are the Son of God, command that these stones become bread." (Matthew 4:1–3)

Here, we find Christ—young, newly commissioned to His ministry, and recently baptized in the Jordan River. He had wandered alone in the wilderness for more than a month, fasting. He now hovered near starvation, languishing in the desert heat without a morsel of food. Then Satan hit Him right between the eyes with not just one, not two, but *three* of the toughest temptations ever.

Satan had a clear strategy, didn't he? The adversary masterfully tempted Christ at the point of His greatest vulnerability. And he does the same with us as well. Like a war-hardened four-star general, he cleverly designs his plots to capitalize on our weaknesses. He relentlessly searches for that tiny chink in our armor and attempts to sabotage us by ambushing us exactly when and where we least expect it.

Christ certainly possessed the power to accept Satan's dare. What could have been wrong with turning a few stones into bread? God wouldn't have wanted His Son to starve to death, would He? But Satan's seemingly harmless challenge hid a deadly snare. He wanted to test Christ to see whether He would use His power for selfish purposes instead of yielding to the will of the Father.

What did Jesus do? We find our answer in Christ's response:

> But He answered and said, "It is written, 'Man shall not live on bread alone, but on every word that proceeds out of the mouth of God.'" (Matthew 4:4)

Because He felt such a fierce hunger, the thought of turning dry, dusty stones into fresh bread must have appealed greatly to the Lord. But instead of succumbing to temptation's siren call, Jesus responded to Satan using a passage from Deuteronomy:

> He humbled you and let you be hungry, and fed you with manna which you did not know, nor did your fathers know, that He might make you understand that *man does not live by bread alone, but man lives by everything that proceeds out of the mouth of the Lord.* (Deuteronomy 8:3, emphasis added)

Jesus compared Satan's temptations to the tests that the disobedient Israelites placed upon God while wandering in the desert for forty years. God's people learned the hard way that genuine faith required them to depend on Yahweh to meet their needs according to *His* timetable, not theirs.

Similarly, Jesus knew that He was called to submit to the Father's will and to allow the Almighty to meet His needs, so He chose to use His power to fulfill the Father's purposes rather than to glorify Himself. Hungry as He was,

Jesus passed up the tempting bread of immediate satisfaction for the more lasting food of obedience to His Father.

A Public Test

The second test was of a public nature. From a perch forty-five stories high, Satan tried to convince Jesus to show off His identity with a sensational "Superman" leap:

> Then the devil took Him into the holy city and had Him stand on the pinnacle of the temple, and said to Him, "If You are the Son of God, throw Yourself down; for it is written, 'He will command His angels concerning You'; and 'On their hands they will bear You up, so that you will not strike Your foot against a stone.'" (Matthew 4:5–6)

A feat of this magnitude would have been a spectacular way for Christ to inaugurate His public ministry. Not only would such an Evel Knievel-style jump have been a real crowd pleaser, it would also have immediately established Jesus as the Messiah that the Jews had been waiting for.

However, instead of trying to please others with death-defying feats of messianic power, Christ sought to please His heavenly Father. So He offered Satan this retort:

> Jesus said to him, "On the other hand, it is written, 'You shall not put the Lord your God to the test.'" (Matthew 4:7)

No doubt, Satan shook His head in disgust at Jesus's righteous answer. What could have been wrong with a little pinnacle jumping? After all, *Satan* would have done it. He loved being the center of attention. But Scripture calls it "presumption" when we flirt with danger in order to prove God's power to rescue us, and the Bible condemns acts of this nature. In the book of Psalms, David asks God to "keep back Your servant from presumptuous sins" (19:13).

Sometimes God expects His children to take risks of faith, but He never asks us to be reckless in order to bring about His divine deliverance. To do so draws attention to ourselves instead of glorifying God. Not only that, but it creates a circus atmosphere in which greater and greater miracles are needed to hold the attention of the crowd.

A Power-Related Test

The third test was of a power-related nature. Furious at being foiled twice, Satan pulled out all the stops to make his last temptation the most extraordinary and difficult to overcome yet. With the flair of a circus ringmaster, he flung open the world's curtains to reveal his showstopper—the most tantalizing temptation of all:

> Again, the devil took Him to a very high mountain and showed Him all the kingdoms of the world and their glory; and he said to Him, "All these things I will give You, if You fall down and worship me." (Matthew 4:8–9)

Satan led Jesus up to the peak of a mountain overlooking the glittering kingdoms of the world. In every direction stretched vast empires waiting to be claimed. The entire world beckoned in the distance, and all of it was

Christ's for the taking.

Christ understood that God planned for Him to rule the kingdoms of the earth, but He also knew that the Father's plan did *not* include Satan's presumptuous offer. So Christ turned down the devil's tempting proposition and, instead, issued him a sharp rebuke:

> Then Jesus said to him, "Go, Satan! For it is written, 'You shall worship the Lord your God, and serve Him only.'" Then the devil left Him; and behold, angels came and began to minister to Him. (Matthew 4:10–11)

Weak though He was from exhaustion and hunger, Jesus refused to give in to Satan's best-laid plans to destroy Him. Disgusted, His accuser finally fled in defeat, and God immediately sent angels to refresh and comfort Jesus.

THREE WISE RESPONSES TO TEMPTATION

Like Christ, all of us face temptations that test our mettle and reveal our character. In some ways, these temptations can be blessings because they reveal the true attitudes of our hearts. Here are three ways that we can respond wisely to temptation.

Don't be alarmed; expect it! Our temptations begin as inner battles of the mind and unseen struggles of the will. When we expect these attacks and prepare to face them, we stay alert for the spiritual battle. The apostle Paul encouraged the Corinthians to keep short accounts with one another in order that "no advantage would be taken of us by Satan, for we are not ignorant of his schemes" (2 Corinthians 2:11).

Do you sometimes find yourself surprised or caught off guard by trials and temptations? If so, how can you better prepare yourself to face them when they come?

_____

_____

_____

_____

_____

Read Ephesians 6:10–17. What weapons and strategies does God provide for you to use in fighting temptation?

_____

_____

_____

_____

_____

How might these weapons and strategies be helpful as you fight temptation? Can you think of specific instances in which you might use them?

_____

_____

_____

_____

_____

Don't be blind; detect it! The adversary has innumerable methods of attack. Satan's covert schemes may blindside you if you're not careful. Ask God to help you detect evil activity around you and to prepare you to confront the accuser's attempts to invade your life. In addition, seek out a trusted

Christian friend who understands the temptations you face. He or she can help keep you in check, support you in prayer, and encourage you when you're prone to temptation.

Can you think of a time when you were blind to Satan's attacks? What happened as a result?

_____

_____

_____

_____

What methods does Satan normally use to attack you and your loved ones? Why do you think he uses these particular methods?

_____

_____

_____

_____

In what ways can you cultivate a deeper spiritual sensitivity so that you can more easily tap into God's power and detect Satan's evil schemes?

_____

_____

_____

_____

Don't try to be clever; reject it! Some believers naively think that they can roll up their spiritual sleeves and challenge the devil to a duel. What a foolish thought! Don't attempt to play clever games with Satan. He's much more powerful than you are in the flesh! You need the Holy Spirit's help to fend off the devil's attacks.

Temptation is like a wild animal; it's not something you can tame. At times, it may seem harmless, but it will *always* possess a killer instinct. You will *never* be able to make it your pet. Instead, do what the apostle James commands: "Submit therefore to God. Resist the devil and he will flee from you" (James 4:7).

What is the greatest temptation you're facing in your life right now? What makes it so difficult to overcome?

_____

_____

_____

_____

As you think about the above situation, in which ways can you submit more fully to God as you face this temptation?

_____

_____

_____

_____

Which of your friends or family members can you trust to keep you accountable to God and resist Satan with regard to this particular temptation?

_____

_____

TAKING TRUTH TO HEART

Tucked away in Hebrews 4, we find some extremely comforting words for those who are determined to get through the tough stuff of temptation. Read this section of Scripture slowly and carefully. Don't miss the power and hope these verses contain!

For we do not have a high priest who cannot sympathize with our weaknesses, but One who has been tempted in all things as we are, yet without sin. Therefore let us draw near with confidence to the throne of grace, so that we may receive mercy and find grace to help in time of need. (Hebrews 4:15–16)

Eugene Peterson paraphrases the same passage this way in *The Message:*

We don't have a priest who is out of touch with our reality. He's been through weakness and testing, experienced it all—all but the sin. So let's walk right up to him and get what he is so ready to give. Take the mercy, accept the help.

How could Jesus have been tempted in all the ways that we have? He lived a short life on earth, taking the journey to the Cross at age thirty-three. He never married, had children, owned a home, or worked in the corporate world. How could He possibly understand the struggles and temptations that we face today in the twenty-first century?

If that's our logic, we're missing something. While Christ may not have experienced every specific temptation that you or I have faced, He was tempted in every arena of His personal and public life, yet He didn't yield to sin. No other human being before or since has been able to withstand the unbridled force of Satan's power. Christ is in touch with our reality.

That's why we can depend on our Savior to get us through the tough stuff of temptation. He's been there. He has felt the sting of rejection and betrayal, yet He has triumphed over evil and the grave. No other person but Jesus could say, "I have thwarted all the attacks of the enemy. When you face your own temptations, you can rely on Me. I have the power that you need. 'Take the mercy, accept the help.'"

two

GETTING THROUGH THE
TOUGH STUFF OF MISUNDERSTANDING

Ralph Waldo Emerson wrote, "To be great is to be misunderstood."[1] Some of us may read that and think, "Wow! If that's true, I must be greater than I thought."

We've all known the pain of hurtful misunderstandings. Perhaps you've tried to reach out to a friend in need who seemed appreciative at the time, but who later told others that you should have minded your own business. Maybe you've tried to improve your relationship with a family member, but that person constantly criticizes you or twists your words to make the situation even worse. Maybe you've gently tried to restore a close Christian friend who was wandering from the faith, but this person rejected your counsel, calling you "legalistic" or "judgmental." Or perhaps you've tried to compliment or encourage someone, but that person didn't receive your words with grace.

We all can remember discussions, meals, dates, trips, holidays, or even entire relationships that have been ruined by misunderstandings. While some disagreements can be cleared up quickly and easily, others linger for years, leaving lasting scars on our hearts and our lives.

The Most Misunderstood Person Ever

Undoubtedly, Jesus Christ was the most misunderstood individual who ever walked this earth. His critics joked about His birth, hinting at illegitimacy. His opposers disputed His heavenly origin and even dared to suggest that Satan, rather than God, provided the basis of His power. Jesus's own people rejected Him, scorned His purpose, and condemned His teachings. In the end, these same people accused Him of blasphemy and turned Him over to be crucified. His crimes? Loving people and demonstrating through His words and miraculous acts that He truly was the Son of God.

The apostle John wrote, "The Light shines in the darkness, and the darkness did not comprehend it" (John 1:5). Christ collided with this uncomprehending darkness at every turn. For a glimpse of what it must have been like to face such unbelief, let's turn to chapter 3 of Mark's gospel. Here, we find four specific groups who misunderstood Jesus's identity and mission.

Misunderstood by the Pharisees

First, Jesus was misunderstood by the Pharisees. His heavenly light blazed a path through the darkness as He taught, helped, and healed others. But, even then, His own people misunderstood Him—especially the religious leaders, whose hatred eclipsed their understanding of His purpose. They watched

Him closely to try to pinpoint a weakness that they could use to bring Him down.

> [Jesus] entered again into a synagogue; and a man was there whose hand was withered. [The Pharisees] were watching Him to see if He would heal him on the Sabbath, so that they might accuse Him. (Mark 3:1–2)

The Pharisees made the rules. As the consummate keepers and enforcers of the law, they represented first-century legalism in full force. They considered their long lists of made-up regulations just as important as the Ten Commandments that God gave to Moses. For example, consider the command, "Remember the Sabbath day, to keep it holy" (Exodus 20:8). The religious leaders added further details to this mandate, such as, "Don't walk on a lawn on the Sabbath. If you do, you'll end up breaking blades of grass, which constitutes work, and absolutely no work is to be done on the Sabbath." How absurd! But no one had the courage or the authority to challenge the religious leaders' silly rules and blatant abuse of power. That is, until Jesus Christ, the Lord of the Sabbath, strode onto the scene.

Jesus knew that the Pharisees had passed a law prohibiting healing on the Sabbath except in the case of a life-or-death situation. He also knew that this law was punishable by death. But He had already informed the self-righteous leaders that "The Sabbath was made for man, and not man for the Sabbath. So the Son of Man is Lord even of the Sabbath" (Mark 2:27–28). He then demonstrated what He meant with an astonishing act of healing:

He said to the man with the withered hand, "Get up and come forward!" And He said to them, "Is it lawful to do good or to do harm on the Sabbath, to save a life or to kill?" But they kept silent. After looking around at them with anger, grieved at their hardness of heart, He said to the man, "Stretch out your hand." And he stretched it out, and his hand was restored. (Mark 3:3–5)

Jesus's pointed question in verse 4 cut a path through the Pharisees' legalistic labyrinth and led them straight to the heart of the issue: their graceless attitudes. The godly compassion that these men should have shown others was replaced with lists of burdensome regulations that the Jewish people found virtually impossible to keep. Jesus responded to this hypocrisy with anger and grief.

Jesus *looked around* (from *periblepomai*, an all-inclusive penetrating look . . .) at the Pharisees *in anger.* . . . It was non-malicious indignation coupled with deep sorrow (grief) at their obstinate insensitivity (*pōrōsei*, "hardening" . . .) to God's mercy and human misery.

When the man held out *his hand* at Jesus' command, it was instantly and *completely restored.* Jesus did not use any visible means that might be construed as "work" on the Sabbath. As Lord of the Sabbath (Mark 2:28) Jesus freed it from legal encumbrances, and in grace delivered this man from his distress.[2]

For the first time in many years, the true purpose of God's Sabbath was revealed in the synagogue as Jesus healed the disfigured man. Few, however, could see that purpose for what it was. The Pharisees felt nothing but murderous hatred for Jesus, whom they considered a dangerous rule breaker. Their response to Christ's gracious healing of the man with the withered hand reflects the hardness of their hearts:

> The Pharisees went out and immediately began conspiring with the Herodians against Him, as to how they might destroy Him. (Mark 3:6)

What were Jesus's purposes in healing the man with the withered hand on the Sabbath?

_____

_____

_____

_____

_____

_____

Why do you think the Pharisees felt so threatened by Christ? How did He challenge their understanding of the Law and the Sabbath?

_____

_____

_____

_____

_____

Misunderstood by His Own People

Second, Jesus was misunderstood by His own people. Mark 3:13–19 describes the manner in which Jesus chose His twelve disciples. After Christ hand-picked these men to follow Him, He returned to his adopted hometown of Capernaum.

> And He came home, and the crowd gathered again, to such an extent that they could not even eat a meal. When His own people heard of this, they went out to take custody of Him; for they were saying, "He has lost His senses." (Mark 3:20–21)

Jesus's own people, who probably had come to Capernaum from Nazareth, could not understand His obvious obsession with His ministry. His involvement with the needs of people had become so consuming, He couldn't even take a moment to eat a piece of bread or a morsel of meat. He was surrounded! Embarrassed by Jesus's passionate fervor, His friends and family decided to "put Him away." Why? They were convinced that He had lost His senses. The Greek translation suggests that they said, "He is beside Himself." How's that for misunderstanding? Jesus was serving His Father with sincerity of heart and with great diligence and passion, and His own people thought He had gone crazy!

No doubt, these friends and family members believed the same thing about the men whom Christ chose as His apostles. Matthew, the tax collector? Andrew and Peter, the fishermen? Not exactly specimens of genius and distinction! These men had left behind their businesses to jump onto the itinerant Teacher's bandwagon. These were the types of people that Jesus was choosing to spend time with. So His hometown folk said, "Let's just put Him away. He'll come to His senses after some time back home." But they missed the point and misunderstood Jesus's mission. To them, Christ's passion hung somewhere between fanaticism and insanity.

Why do you think the religious leaders and Jesus's own people misunderstood His call and His passion for ministry?

_____

_____

_____

_____

_____

_____

_____

Consider a more modern example. The closer Thomas Edison came to inventing the incandescent light bulb, the less he ate and slept. He left meals untouched. Lamps in his shop remained lit for days and nights at a time. Yet, after more than seven hundred failed experiments, his dream of an incandescent light bulb became reality. Every time you and I flip a light switch, we should say, "Thanks, Mr. Edison. You did it. You believed in your idea. You stayed at it day after day and night after night, and as a result, I'll never be in the dark." But what about the people in Edison's day? They grew a little concerned about him too. Because of his passionate pursuit of his goal, he was viewed as eccentric, maybe even a little crazy at times.

Describe a time when you have felt misunderstood by those around you. Did you follow your call, idea, or dream, even when others opposed or doubted you? If so, do you feel you made the right choice by going against the crowd?

_____

_____

_____

_____

Misunderstood by the Scribes

Third, Jesus was misunderstood by the scribes. When they heard what was happening, a delegation of legal experts came from Jerusalem to investigate Jesus. They made this pronouncement: "He is possessed by Beelzebul, and He casts out demons by the ruler of the demons" (Mark 3:22).

GETTING TO THE ROOT

The spelling "Beelzebul" (also "Beelzebub") came into English translations from the Latin Bible (the Vulgate) which derived it from the Hebrew word *Baalzebub* meaning "Lord of the flies," the name of an ancient Canaanite deity.[3] This term can also be translated "the prince of demons."[4] By using this term, the Pharisees falsely insinuated that Jesus's power came from Satan rather than from God.

Jesus didn't stop the Pharisees from plotting His death. He didn't argue with His old friends from Nazareth who suggested that He was crazy. But when the so-called experts in the Law, the scribes, made the blatant, blasphemous accusation that His power came from Satan and not from God, Jesus strongly rebuked them, pointing out the fallacy of their argument.

And He called them to Himself and began speaking to
them in parables, "How can Satan cast out Satan? If a kingdom is divided against itself, that kingdom cannot stand. If
a house is divided against itself, that house will not be able
to stand. If Satan has risen up against himself and is divided,
he cannot stand, but he is finished!" (Mark 3:23–26)

No doubt, the scribes' jaws dropped as Jesus stopped their argument in its
tracks. Mark doesn't mention what these leaders did next. Most likely, they
recognized that they had been beaten at their own game and, afraid to challenge Jesus further, stormed away in anger and humiliation.

Why do you think Jesus issued such a strong rebuke?

_____

_____

_____

_____

_____

Based on Jesus's example, when is it appropriate for us to take action against false accu-
sations, and when is it appropriate to quietly accept a differing opinion? What qualities
or motives should characterize our response in each case?

_____

_____

_____

_____

_____

What other principles can you draw from Jesus's response?

_____

_____

_____

_____

_____

Misunderstood by His Family

Last, Jesus was misunderstood even by His own family.

> Then His mother and His brothers arrived, and standing outside they sent word to Him and called Him. A crowd was sitting around Him, and they said to Him, "Behold, Your mother and Your brothers are outside looking for You." (Mark 3:31–32)

Most Bible scholars agree that Jesus's family waited outside and called for Him because they, too, believed that he had lost His mind. They wanted to talk some sense into Him—try to get Him to come back home, take back His old job at the carpentry shop, and forget all this foolish talk about being the Messiah.

Jesus must have grieved when He realized that even His own mother and brothers couldn't understand His passion for ministering to the lost and hurting. His family still seemed to be skeptical about His call. Despite Christ's hurt, however, He used this misunderstanding as an opportunity to assert His kinship with all those who do the will of God:

Answering them, He said, "Who are My mother and My brothers?" Looking about at those who were sitting around Him, He said, "Behold My mother and My brothers! For whoever does the will of God, he is My brother and sister and mother." (Mark 3:33–35)

Why do you think Jesus's own mother and brothers were skeptical about His ministry?

What can we learn about the kingdom of God from Jesus's reply to His family in Mark 3:33–35? Based on this, to whom should we turn when our closest friends or family misunderstand our ministry or mission?

TAKING TRUTH TO HEART

In every family circle, every marriage, every group of friends, and every workplace, misunderstandings occur that can eat away at our relationships like corrosive acid. The longer we leave these disagreements unattended, the more destructive they become. In order to help you resolve such issues, ask yourself these three questions the next time you face a difficult misunderstanding.

Ask yourself who. Who is responsible for the problem? Usually both parties have contributed to the situation in some way. Consider the source and the context. Is it possible that you have overreacted to the other person's words or actions? Try to see the situation from the other person's perspective and attempt to talk to that person about the problem with understanding and patience.

If the problem continues, ask yourself why. Why has this misunderstanding occurred? Why are you upset about it? What is the root cause? Is it something that the other person did, or is it possible that you caused the problem without realizing it? Perhaps this situation represents a blind spot in your life, an area in which you need to grow. If so, you may need the perspective of an objective third party to help you solve the problem. Do your best to be honest with yourself and the others involved, and try to come to a resolution.

After you resolve the problem, ask yourself what. What have you learned? What could you do differently next time? In what ways can you and the other person benefit from this experience? What did you learn about yourself from this situation? As you evaluate what happened, recognize that you and the other party graciously need to forgive each other and move on in order for your relationship to be restored.

Think about your God-given passions for your life and ministry. Has everyone you've encountered been supportive and encouraging of how you choose to live those out? Is there anyone you need to respectfully confront, or anyone you need to quietly forgive?

Spend some time talking with God about your specific area of need. Ask Him to give you His wisdom in how to handle it. He promises to do just that (see James 1:5).

To be great is to be misunderstood, but to be even greater is to forgive those who have misunderstood you. Not only was Jesus the greatest and most misunderstood man ever to live—He also was the most forgiving. He offered forgiveness to others even as He hung in excruciating pain on the cross (see Luke 23:34). Trusting in Him doesn't prevent us from encountering disagreements, but it does enable us to survive them, move past them, and get on with our lives. By following His example of forgiveness, we can repair the damage done by life's inevitable misunderstandings.

three

Getting Through the Tough Stuff of Anxiety

Americans once listed the following as their top ten fears:

1. Speaking before a group
2. Heights
3. Insects and bugs
4. Financial problems
5. Deep water

6. Sickness
7. Death
8. Flying
9. Loneliness
10. Dogs[1]

While this list may not reflect all of your greatest fears, reading it probably made your heart beat a little faster. All of the items in this list have one thing in common: when we grapple with them, we're forced to realize we're not in control of our own lives. We all struggle in situations in which we can't ensure a positive outcome. We prefer to take matters into our own hands and try to solve our problems our own way. But when we approach our lives with the mistaken notion that we're in control, we short-circuit the work that God wants to do in us.

In contrast, when we humbly acknowledge our anxieties and fears and depend upon God to lead us through them, we demonstrate what it means to have an active, living faith—a faith that holds fast even when we face the anxiety of loneliness, deep water, or public speaking!

IDENTIFYING ANXIETY

Webster defines *anxiety* as "painful or apprehensive uneasiness of mind usually over an impending or anticipated ill; . . . an abnormal and overwhelming sense of apprehension and fear often marked by physiological signs (as sweating, tension, and increased pulse) . . . and by self-doubt about one's capacity to cope with it."[2] That's quite a definition! More simply, we could consider *anxiety* to be mental, emotional, or spiritual strangulation. Mild anxiety makes our insides churn; great anxiety causes us to panic.

GETTING TO THE ROOT

The word *anxious* in the New Testament comes from the Greek verb *merimnaō*, meaning "to be divided or distracted." In Latin, the same word is translated *anxius*, but with the added nuance of "choking" or "strangling." This same negative connotation colors the German word *wurgen*, from which we get the English word "worry." Since ancient times, worry's nature hasn't changed. It still strangles. It still chokes out life.

What would you say are your greatest fears? Why do you think you fear these particular things or situations so much?

_____

_____

_____

_____

What situations in your life right now make you the most anxious?

_____

_____

_____

_____

How does this anxiousness tend to manifest itself in your life?

_____

_____

_____

_____

As we explore a vignette from the lives of two sisters from the town of Bethany, we'll discover how our worries can affect our worship.

JESUS VISITS MARTHA AND MARY

Let's meet the two women at the heart of the story:

Now as they were traveling along, He entered a village; and a woman named Martha welcomed Him into her

home. She had a sister called Mary, who was seated at the
Lord's feet, listening to His word. (Luke 10:38–39)

Notice the difference in the two sisters' personalities? Martha, most likely the older sister, came to the door to welcome Jesus. No doubt, she was pleased to see Him, and she invited Him inside. But instead of sitting down and asking Him about His trip, she frantically began making a mental to-do list: choose a main course for dinner, dress and cook the meat, bake the bread, set the table, and put the house in order. After all, *Jesus* was there!

Scripture mentions this particular Mary, the sister of Martha and Lazarus, three times (see Luke 10:39; John 11:32, 12:3). Each time we meet her, she's kneeling in worship at the Savior's feet. Her physical position reflects her spiritual posture, and both reveal the nature of Mary's close relationship with Jesus. She recognized Him as the Son of God and humbly worshiped Him as such. In addition, she seemed to understand that Christ's mission on earth included not just glory, but extraordinary sacrifice.

Martha, meanwhile, busied herself in the kitchen, where she wasn't just whipping up a spectacular meal for her unexpected houseguest—she was also working up quite an attitude. Author Ken Gire describes the thoughts and emotions that may have flooded Martha's mind as she slaved away in the kitchen:

> *I can't believe Mary isn't in here helping,* she thinks. Martha pushes a fist into the dough. *She should be in here.* Another fist into the dough. *We could get this done in half the time.* She pulls and mashes, pulls and mashes. *You know, I'd like to hear*

what he has to say, too, but somebody's got to fix dinner. Martha reaches for some flour and flings it on the lump. *They could at least come in here while they talk.* She works the flour into the expanding loaf. *I can't believe he just lets her sit there.* Another fist into the dough. *Here I am in the kitchen, sweating, working my fingers to the bone . . . doesn't he care?*[3]

Finally, the dam holding Martha's pent-up emotions burst. Angrily tossing her lump of dough aside, she stormed into the living room to give Jesus a piece of her mind. Can't you just picture her standing there in a dirty apron with her hands on her hips, face sweaty and hair tousled, letting the angry words fly? Luke describes the scene this way:

> But Martha was distracted with all her preparations; and she came up to Him and said, "Lord, do You not care that my sister has left me to do all the serving alone? Then tell her to help me." (Luke 10:40)

Instead of bringing her grievance to Mary in private, Martha went straight to Jesus, fully expecting Him to take her side and order Mary to help her. But don't miss the first part of Martha's question: "Lord, do You not *care* . . . ?" The fact that Martha accused Jesus of not caring indicates that her anger toward Mary had spilled over to include Him, as well.

Read Luke 10:40 again. Have you ever felt the way Martha did in the passage? Describe the circumstances and what happened.

_____

_____

_____

_____

We might have expected a strong rebuke from Jesus after Martha's outburst. But instead of responding to her harshly, Jesus disarmed her anger with a gentle reply. As He spoke, He probably put His arm around her shoulders and drew her near to comfort and calm her, demonstrating that He truly did care for His friend Martha.

> But the Lord answered and said to her, "Martha, Martha, you are worried and bothered about so many things; but only one thing is necessary, for Mary has chosen the good part, which shall not be taken away from her." (Luke 10:41–42)

What did Christ mean when He said that Mary had "chosen the good part"? In Greek, the term "part" is often used to describe a portion of food. Here, Jesus used the term as a word play to contrast the spiritual nourishment He offered with the physical nourishment that Martha had been busy preparing. The best part of the meal wasn't being served in the kitchen—it could be found only at the feet of Christ. And Mary was the only one sitting there, ready to receive it.

Jesus chose this teachable moment to reveal a vital truth about Himself and the kingdom of God.

In contrast to life's many responsibilities, Jesus says that only a few things are really necessary. And, when you get right down to it, only one. The one thing necessary, the one thing of eternal value, the one thing that shall not be taken away, is the time we spend seated at Christ's feet, looking into His eyes with adoration and listening to His Word in submission.[4]

TAKING TRUTH TO HEART

Martha *worried*. As the "worker bee" of the family, she always wanted to do things the right way. She graciously opened her home to Jesus but then busied herself with the dinner details. She concerned herself with propriety, appearance, timeliness, and orderliness, but in the process, she lost sight of what mattered most—spending time with Jesus.

Mary, on the other hand, *worshiped*. She was content to stop doing and just be. She was less concerned with doing things right than she was with doing the right things. She understood that Christ's death was nearing, and she knew that this could be her last opportunity to spend time with Him, so she tuned out the distractions around her and focused all her attention on Jesus. While Martha rushed frantically around the house, Mary "chose the good part," and Christ honored her for making the right choice.

What things in your life tend to crowd out spending time with Jesus?

_____

_____

_____

_____

Read John 17:3 and Philippians 3:8. What does God say is the purpose of your life?

_____

_____

_____

_____

Do the things that crowd out time with Jesus indicate that your purposes may differ at times from God's? Explain.

_____

_____

_____

_____

How can you better align your life purpose with God's purpose for you?

_____

_____

_____

_____

In the past, we may have been tempted to criticize Martha, but before we do so, let's put ourselves in her place. Most of us probably fit the description of Martha better than that of Mary. We spend much more time working than we do worshiping. Often, we prefer to busy ourselves with "kingdom work" rather than sitting at the feet of Christ. In fact, we even get angry when other church members sit back and relax, forcing a small number of people to do all the important, difficult, and often-thankless ministry work. We secretly tend to label the "Marys" around us as unmotivated, lazy, or unreliable.

Read Luke 10:41–42 again carefully. What words or phrases does Jesus use to describe Martha? What does He say about Mary in these verses?

_____

_____

_____

_____

Which sister do you most identify with? Are you more of an active worrier, like Martha, or a quiet worshiper like Mary?

_____

_____

_____

_____

How did Jesus help to shift Martha's perspective from the temporal to the eternal?

_____

_____

_____

_____

If you were to choose the "good part," like Mary, in your own life, what would that look like? How would that affect your current values and priorities?

_____

_____

_____

_____

Four Effects of Anxiety

Anxiety affects us in four distinct ways:

It highlights the human viewpoint and strangles the divine, making us fearful. When we worry, we become so acutely aware of human events surrounding us that God's perspective often gets overlooked. Worry keeps our focus on ourselves, which puts us on edge.

Anxiety chokes our ability to distinguish the incidental from the essential, so we get distracted. In the midst of the worrisome details of life, we tend to focus on our fears, doubts, tasks, expectations, and pressures. Eventually, we lose sight of what really matters. We become distracted by the unimportant and, as a result, we neglect the things that are truly significant.

Anxiety twists so many worries around our hearts that we cannot relax, so we become unfruitful. Fruitful people are usually relaxed people who trust God and allow Him to carry their burdens and anxieties. Spiritually unproductive people, on the other hand, tend to get themselves tied up in knots, allowing incidental worries to entangle their minds like thorns.

Anxiety siphons our energy and joy, making us judgmental and negative rather than accepting. We become negative when worry wins the battle and, inevitably, we start to take our anxiety out on others. Worry operates like bad cholesterol, hardening the arteries of our spiritual hearts and clogging the flow of love and grace toward people. Eventually, as the thorns and thistles intensify, we can become bitter, narrow people who don't reflect the joy and love of Christ.

How can we fend off these negative effects of anxiety? By clinging to God's Word and allowing our paths to be illuminated by His truth. Our first clue to battling worry appears in the book of Philippians:

> Be anxious for nothing, but in everything by prayer and supplication with thanksgiving let your requests be made known to God. And the peace of God, which surpasses all comprehension, will guard your hearts and your minds in Christ Jesus. (Philippians 4:6–7)

Be anxious for *nothing?* What could be more difficult than that? Letting go of our worry seems impossible, but God's Word promises us that it's not.

How can we tackle anxiety and gain peace? By praying about everything. By supplicating and submitting our lives to God. By thanking Him for everything that happens in our lives—the good *and* the bad. By trusting that His will is greater than our will and His plans are greater than our plans. When we do all of these things, what do we gain as a result? Supernatural spiritual peace that surpasses all understanding.

four

Getting Through the Tough Stuff of Shame

Do you remember the television commercials that called hypertension "the silent killer"? This disease, which can prove fatal, afflicts millions who do not know they have it. Undiagnosed and untreated, hypertension can slowly lead to heart attack, stroke, kidney failure, and blindness.

A silent spiritual killer exists, too. It lies undiagnosed and untreated in millions of Christians. Over time, it produces deadly spiritual symptoms: constant discouragement, a lack of self-worth, hopelessness about ever being good enough for God, a sense of disconnection from God, and the absence of joy. It blocks us from the abundant life Jesus came to provide. The name of this silent spiritual killer? Shame. The only effective treatment? Deeply experiencing the grace of God.

Jesus never did anything that He needed to be ashamed of, but that didn't keep Him from willingly taking our shame upon Himself at the Cross.

He sacrificed His life in order to reconcile us to God. The holy and perfect One, the utterly sinless One, bore our sins on the Cross. He suffered under the crushing weight of every wicked act ever committed, all of mankind's darkest thoughts and actions, at Calvary. He refused to run from the shame that we so often try to elude. Instead, He chose the way of the Cross, where He took our guilt and shame on Himself in order to redeem and release us from our sin. His forgiving grace reaches into one of the darkest areas of our lives—the area where we hide our shame.

SHAME: AN AGONY ALL ITS OWN

What exactly is shame? Webster defines it as "a painful emotion caused by consciousness of guilt, shortcoming, or impropriety; . . . a condition of humiliating disgrace or disrepute."[1] Whereas guilt signals our awareness of our sin, shame is the feeling of embarrassment we have when our sinful actions and our guilt become evident to others. Shame manifests itself in our relationships, causing us to act differently around those we've hurt and those we feel might judge us for our sin.

Shame attempts to write its destructive message on the pages of our hearts. When thoughts and feelings of unworthiness flood our souls, we need the truth of Scripture to help us erase the message of shame and instead write "GRACE" in large letters on the tablets of our lives.

What situations or sins in your life have caused you the most shame?

_____

_____

_____

What was it about these particular situations that caused you to feel this way?

_____

_____

_____

_____

In John 8, Christ freed a woman from her shame, forgave her sin, and changed her life forever. As we examine His actions, we'll learn principles for getting past our own shame and experiencing God's freedom and grace in our lives.

An Adulteress and Her Accusers

Our story begins as Christ entered the temple to teach the people:

> Early in the morning He came again into the temple, and
> all the people were coming to Him; and He sat down and
> began to teach them. (John 8:2)

As the first rays of sunlight stole over Jerusalem, the early risers among the Jews swarmed up the narrow streets of the city toward the temple. They gathered in a large crowd in the brisk morning air, awaiting more life-changing teaching from the mouth of Jesus. So He began to share words of eternal life with them.

But suddenly, the scene changed. The calm setting was shattered by a handful of men with hearts dead set on destruction:

> The scribes and the Pharisees brought a woman caught in adultery, and having set her in the center of the court, they said to Him, "Teacher, this woman has been caught in adultery, in the very act. Now in the Law Moses commanded us to stone such women; what then do You say?" They were saying this, testing Him, so that they might have grounds for accusing Him. (John 8:3–6)

If you've ever been in a situation in which the atmosphere changed radically from one instant to the next, you know how Jesus and His eager listeners must have felt at that moment. Imagine the scene. Their early morning gathering of teaching and worship had suddenly been interrupted by a shocking spectacle. Christ stopped speaking in midsentence; gasps went up all around as a disheveled woman was dragged into cen-

GETTING TO THE ROOT

The word *caught* in John 8:4, from the Greek word *katalambano*, means "to lay hold of, seize."[2] This term suggests that the scribes and Pharisees had actually pulled the woman from her sexual partner, seized her, and dragged her away. There was absolutely no question that this woman had committed the sin of which she had been accused.

ter court. The Pharisees roughly shoved her before Christ, where she crumpled into a heap of disgrace and despair.

If the woman had looked up, the people around her would have seen the terror and shame in her dark eyes. But she kept her flushed face hidden behind her mane of long, matted hair. Her bruised face, arms, and legs bore the marks of her struggle. Her breathing was panicked and erratic. A half-moan escaped from her lips.

The woman knew the penalty for adultery. If the Pharisees had their way, she soon would be stoned to death. She had no reason to believe her life would be spared. But in her heart, perhaps she lifted up a silent, desperate plea to God. Maybe, just maybe, He might save her life.

If you were this woman, caught in sin and brought before Jesus by the Pharisees, what emotions do you think you would be experiencing?

In case you hadn't already noticed, another problem has surfaced in our story. Where was the woman's lover? If the Pharisees had caught her "in the very act," then that assumes that they had caught her partner in the very act also. He, too, should have been convicted and sentenced to die for committing adultery. His absence here was just as conspicuous as her presence. The Pharisees may have even planted one of their own men in this adulterous situation as part of their larger plan to trap Jesus. William Barclay explains the dilemma these religious leaders had created for Jesus:

If he said that the woman ought to be stoned to death, two things followed. First, he would lose the name he had gained for love and for mercy and never again would be called the friend of sinners. Second, he would come into collision with the Roman law, for the Jews had no power to pass or carry out the death sentence on anyone. If he said that the woman should be pardoned, it could immediately be said that he was teaching men to break the Law of Moses, and that he was condoning and even encouraging people to commit adultery. That was the trap in which the scribes and Pharisees sought to entrap Jesus.[3]

Justice or mercy? Either answer was a snare. The Pharisees thought they had Jesus cornered. They smugly thought, *Aha! There's no way He can worm His way out of this one.* Instead of answering their questions, however, Jesus did a surprising thing:

> But Jesus stooped down and with His finger wrote on the ground. (John 8:6)

What did Jesus write? Was He just casually doodling in the dust while He collected His thoughts? Probably not. The Greek term used here for "wrote" suggests something more:

> The normal Greek word for *to write* is *graphein*; but here the word used is *katagraphein*, which can mean *to write down a*

record against someone. . . . It may be that Jesus was confronting those self-confident sadists with the record of their own sins.[4]

In all of the New Testament, the word for this specific act ("writing down against") appears only in John 8:6. Jesus's calm persona and His unusual tactic of writing in the dirt only stirred the Pharisees into more of a frenzy. But they had underestimated Jesus. They were about to discover just whom they were dealing with.

Her Advocate and His Approach

The Pharisees kept pestering Jesus for His answer. But with a single spoken sentence, Jesus sent these bloodthirsty religious leaders reeling.

> But when they persisted in asking Him, He straightened
> up, and said to them, "He who is without sin among you,
> let him be the first to throw a stone at her." Again He
> stooped down and wrote on the ground. (John 8:7–8)

Jesus's pointed words punctured even the rock-hard hearts of the Pharisees. The word order of the Greek indicates the emphasis—and impact—of His challenge. Literally, Jesus said, "The *sinless* one of you first, on her let him cast a stone" (emphasis added). That meant none of these men had a right to lift a finger against the woman. Jesus had checkmate against the Pharisees, and they knew it. They had no choice but to concede that Christ had beaten them at their own game.

When they heard it, they began to go out one by one, beginning with the older ones, and He was left alone, and the woman, where she was, in the center of the court. (John 8:9)

Peter Marshall described this dramatic scene:

Looking into their faces, Christ sees into the yesterdays that lie deep in the pools of memory and conscience.
He sees into their very hearts, and that moving finger writes on . . .

Idolater . . .

Liar . . .

Drunkard . . .

Murderer . . .

Adulterer . . .

There is the thud of stone after stone falling on the pavement.
Not many of the Pharisees are left.
One by one, they creep away—like animals—slinking into the shadows . . .

shuffling off into the crowded streets to lose themselves in the multitudes.[5]

What do you think the Pharisees and scribes expected Jesus to say when they questioned Him about the fate of the woman caught in adultery? Why?

What spiritual point did Jesus make with His answer?

Though her accusers had dropped their death stones and fled, the humiliated woman remained rooted to the ground in her fear and guilt. The embers of her public shame still burned within her, kindling feelings of unworthiness and self-doubt. Even though none of her accusers remained to condemn her, she blamed and condemned herself. But Jesus, the perfect, holy Son of God, did just the opposite:

> Straightening up, Jesus said to her, "Woman, where are they? Did no one condemn you?" She said, "No one, Lord." And Jesus said, "I do not condemn you, either. Go. From now on sin no more." (John 8:10–11)

Christ, the only sinless person in the world, the only One qualified to condemn this woman, didn't. Instead of demanding that she pay for her sin, Jesus kindly and graciously restored her, setting her free from the painful shackles of her shame. With honesty and compassion, Jesus chose to clothe the "scarlet woman" with the white robes of His forgiveness, righteousness, and love. When He looked at her, He saw not a naked, scared, bruised adulteress, but a precious daughter of the King.

By saying what He said and refusing to condemn the woman, what spiritual truths and priorities did Jesus illustrate to the woman, the crowd, and the Pharisees?

_____

_____

_____

_____

TAKING TRUTH TO HEART

Jesus set the woman free from her shame, and He will do the same for you when you accept His offer of forgiveness. On the cross, He lifted the yoke of your sin and shame onto His own shoulders so that you no longer have to bear it. In place of those feelings of shame and unworthiness, He offers you His lovingkindness, peace, restoration, and sense of worth. As Paul wrote, "He [God the Father] made Him [Jesus] who knew no sin to be sin on our behalf, so that we might become the righteousness of God in Him ." (2 Corinthians 5:21). In Christ, you are the very righteousness of God. You're a joint heir with Him to the riches of God's kingdom.

Based on His interaction with the woman, what do you think Jesus would say to you regarding the situations in your life that have caused you shame? (Recall the things you listed earlier in the chapter.)

_____

_____

_____

_____

_____

_____

If you haven't already done so, take time now to pray about these situations and offer them up to the Lord.

_____

_____

_____

_____

_____

How can you show that you've accepted God's forgiveness and applied Jesus's freeing words to your own life?

_____

_____

_____

_____

_____

_____

Two Principles for Overcoming Shame

From Jesus's interaction with the woman and the Pharisees, we can glean two principles regarding shame and how we can overcome it.

Those who are not qualified to condemn you will. You can count on it! Like the Pharisees, certain people will try to set traps for you and throw stones at you. Do your best to stay away from those legalistic, destructive people. Instead, seek friends who will encourage you, support you, and provide loving accountability for you. In addition, be willing and available to offer hope, help, and a spiritual perspective to others.

The One who is qualified to condemn you won't. Stay close to Him and remain in His Word. By keeping your relationship with God strong, you'll be able to fend off negative messages and feelings of shame that the world will try to impose upon you. Like the woman in John 8, you'll experience healing and restoration through Christ so you, too, can "go and sin no more."

In the past, have you tended to trap or condemn others for their sin instead of offering mercy and trying to help them gain restoration? Do you currently? If so, how can you change your attitudes and actions to better reflect what you've learned from John 8?

_____

_____

_____

_____

_____

_____

_____

To All Weighed Down by Shame

Each of us has experienced moments when we were "caught in the very act" of some sin or another. It may not have been adultery, but it was sin just the same. And we will face similar situations in the future in which we will make the wrong decisions, say the wrong words, or do the wrong things.

Like the woman in John 8, we, too, will face rock throwers who will try to condemn us. For your own sake, stay away from "Pharisees" like this. Don't allow them to use you for their spiritual target practice. Instead, draw near and confess your sin and your shame to the One who forgives you instead of condemning you. In the book of Romans, the apostle Paul declared, "Therefore there is now no condemnation for those who are in Christ Jesus" (Romans 8:1).

If you had been in the place of the woman caught in her sin and dragged by the Pharisees before Jesus on that morning, His words to you would have been the same: "I do not condemn you, either. Go. From now on sin no more." This means that instead of living a defeated life, mired in your shame, you're empowered to live a victorious life of freedom and grace through Christ.

five

GETTING THROUGH THE
TOUGH STUFF OF DOUBT

Throughout church history, opinions and attitudes about doubt have varied greatly. To some believers, doubt represents the worst kind of blasphemy. The courageous reformer Martin Luther, for example, "felt that he had no greater enemy than doubt." He considered it a "monster of uncertainty" and a "gospel of despair."[1]

Others, however, argue that doubt is natural to humanity and is an essential part of any intelligent pursuit of the truth. Tennyson wrote, "There lives more faith in honest doubt, believe me, than in half the creeds."[2]

While we may not all agree on the subject of doubt, most of us have experienced it at one time or another. Clearly, it's possible for even faithful, mature believers to struggle with doubt. Our faith in God requires us to trust in things unseen. It also requires us to accept the fact that some aspects of God's truth and His kingdom will remain mysteries until we come face to face with Him in eternity.

Scripture tells us that overcoming our doubts requires a heaping dose of faith. The author of the book of Hebrews wrote:

> Now faith is the assurance of things hoped for, the conviction of things not seen. . . . And without faith it is impossible to please Him, for he who comes to God must believe that He is and that He is a rewarder of those who seek Him. (11:1, 6)

GETTING TO THE ROOT

The Greek word *diakrinō*, translated "doubt," has several nuances of meaning in the New Testament, including "to distinguish," "to judge," "to dispute," "to have misgivings," and "to waver."[3]

Did you catch that? Without faith it is *impossible* to please God. And without faith, it's impossible to overcome doubt.

Several people in the Bible expressed true faith in God, but they also had doubts about that faith from time to time. One is the desperate father described in Mark 9 who brought his demon-possessed son to Jesus for healing. Just listen to the combination of heart-wrenching despair and anxious hope in this father's voice:

> They brought the boy to [Jesus]. When he saw Him, immediately the spirit threw him into a convulsion, and falling to the ground, he began rolling around and foaming at the mouth. And He asked his father, "How long has this been

happening to him?" And he said, "From childhood. It has often thrown him both into the fire and into the water to destroy him. *But if You can do anything, take pity on us and help us!*" And Jesus said to him, "'If You can?' All things are possible to him who believes." Immediately the boy's father cried out and said, *"I do believe; help my unbelief."* (Mark 9:20–24, emphasis added)

Here we find as raw an expression of honest faith and real doubt as we'll discover anywhere. Ever since a demonic spirit had first possessed his son, this poor father and his child had suffered tremendously. The youth was now mute, unable to say a word. He suffered frequently from severe convulsions that left him writhing on the ground, foaming at the mouth like a rabid animal. The demon inside him often tried to force the boy to burn or drown himself.

Some tried to ignore the boy's public outbursts, while others talked about him and his family behind their backs. Old friends stopped coming around. Life quickly grew ugly for this father and his son.

Against this backdrop of personal torment, the boy's father struggled to maintain his faith. He was familiar with Jesus's ministry, and he trusted that the Lord could heal his son; otherwise, he wouldn't have bothered bringing the boy to Christ. The father *wanted* to believe—he just needed a faith boost. He wanted desperately to trust that all of his son's pain and anguish could end with a few healing words from the mouth of Jesus.

TAKING TRUTH TO HEART

Though few of us have experienced life with a demon-possessed child, we have been through circumstances that severely tried our faith. We've all faced problems that sent doubts fissuring deep into the sacred beliefs that we once considered rock solid and beyond question. In fact, you may be facing a faith-testing trial right now. In such moments of anguish and turmoil, we can cry out, "Lord, I do believe; please help my unbelief!"

Which situations in your life have caused you to doubt God? Why do you think these particular situations caused you to doubt?

_____

_____

_____

_____

_____

_____

Were you able to work through those feelings of doubt? Why or why not?

_____

_____

_____

_____

_____

WHEN DOUBTS EMERGE

Doubt plagues us when we reach the limits of our understanding. It hangs over our heads when we encounter a sudden, unexpected calamity that seems to have no purpose except to cause us grief and pain. It lingers in our minds when we pray for something and exactly the opposite occurs. We face it when our friends or professors share philosophies that seem to contradict the tenets of our faith. We feel it when a respected friend, pastor, or mentor denies God's existence and walks away from the faith. We experience it when we make sacrifices to follow God and then seem to suffer miserably for it.

Circumstances such as these raise all sorts of questions in our minds. Should we try to ignore our doubts? Should we be afraid to ask tough questions? Should we stuff our conflicting thoughts and emotions inside and pretend that we're fine? Absolutely not.

> Questions . . . are the grappling hooks by which the sheer summits of truth can be scaled.
>
> Consequently, those hooks, however sharp, should not be feared. Neither should they be discouraged. For questions are the very hooks by which a person climbs from doubt to faith.[4]

People who honestly face the questions raised by doubt are what author Daniel Taylor calls "reflective Christians."

> The reflective person is, first and foremost, a question asker—one who finds in every experience and assertion

something that requires further investigation. He or she is a stone turner, attracted to the creepy-crawly things that live under rocks and behind human pronouncements. The writer of Ecclesiastes was such a person: "I directed my mind to know, to investigate, and to seek wisdom and an explanation . . ." (Ecclesiastes 7:25).[5]

Do you agree with the above assertions that asking tough questions is a healthy part of seeking to know the truth? Why or why not?

_____

_____

_____

_____

_____

_____

Has there ever been a time in your own life when your questions led you to a deeper understanding of God? If so, describe your experience.

_____

_____

_____

_____

_____

_____

Reflective Christians aren't afraid to take up their grappling hooks and do some rock climbing and stone turning of their own. Jesus had a disciple named Thomas who definitely fit this description.

Thomas has been stuck with the unfortunate label "Doubting Thomas" for generations. However, this really isn't a fair nickname. "Reflective Thomas" would be a more appropriate moniker. Why? Let's grab our grappling hooks and investigate.

WHY THOMAS STRUGGLED

Thomas was a thinker. He had the courage to question, to admit his struggles, and to raise his hand and say, "Wait a minute! I don't understand what you just said. How could that be true? That makes no sense to me at all." But Thomas had faithfully committed himself to following Jesus and was even prepared to die with Him, as we find in John 11.

Two days after hearing of His friend Lazarus's illness, Jesus announced to His disciples, "Let us go to Judea again" (John 11:7). But the Twelve knew this trip would be dangerous and immediately tried to dissuade Him from going:

> The disciples said to Him, "Rabbi, the Jews were just now
> seeking to stone You, and are You going there again?" (11:8)

The disciples feared not only for Jesus's life, but for their own. But Thomas courageously stepped forward to go with Jesus, even if it meant his own death. This brave disciple's words also reminded the others of their commitment:

> Therefore Thomas, who is called Didymus ["The Twin"],
> said to his fellow disciples, "Let us also go, so that we may
> die with Him." (11:16)

Thomas said *that?* The one whose nickname has made him a paragon of supposed doubt? Yes. The truth is, Thomas expressed great courage and faith in Christ at many points in his life. Remember, his comment wasn't an idle boast from someone who knew that Jesus would soon raise Lazarus from the dead. Thomas honestly believed that he and the others were returning to Judea to die. But he committed himself to standing by Jesus, no matter the cost.

We find another glimpse of Thomas's reflective nature at the Last Supper, recorded in chapters 13 and 14 of John's gospel. The disciples' stomachs churned throughout the meal as Jesus made upsetting pronouncements such as these: "He who eats My bread has lifted up his heel against Me" (13:18), "Truly, truly, I say to you, that one of you will betray Me" (13:21), and "Where I go, you cannot follow Me now; but you will follow later" (13:36). Christ's words in chapter 14 about the disciples knowing their way to His Father's house only caused more confusion:

> "Do not let your heart be troubled; believe in God, believe also in Me. In My Father's house are many dwelling places; if it were not so, I would have told you; for I go to prepare a place for you. If I go and prepare a place for you, I will come again and receive you to Myself, that where I am, there you may be also. And you know the way where I am going." Thomas said to Him, *"Lord, we do not know where You are going, how do we know the way?"* (John 14:1–5, emphasis added)

This disciple, classified over the years as a pessimist, probably should be considered more of a realist. He wasn't afraid to ask questions that would help him understand the person and mission of Christ more clearly. Jesus had said that the disciples knew where He was going, but Thomas hadn't the first clue as to what Jesus meant, and he wasn't afraid to say so. In this case, Thomas's literal-minded question was rewarded by a profound theological answer that has become one of the most-cited verses in Scripture:

> Jesus said to him, "*I am the way*, and the truth, and the life;
> no one comes to the Father but through Me." (John 14:6,
> emphasis added)

Maybe you've noticed an important truth here: the questions Thomas raised led to some of the most incredible answers and insights into God's kingdom that Jesus ever offered. If it weren't for Thomas and his reflective nature, we wouldn't have a window into these extraordinary dialogues and profound theological truths.

WHEN THOMAS DOUBTED

Now, let's journey over to John 20, where we find Thomas's famous expression of doubt over the disciples' announcement that they had seen the risen Christ.

> But Thomas, one of the twelve, called Didymus, was not
> with them when Jesus came. So the other disciples were
> saying to him, "We have seen the Lord!" But he said to
> them, "*Unless I see in His hands the imprint of the nails, and put*

my finger into the place of the nails, and put my hand into His side,
I will not believe." (John 20:24–25, emphasis added)

Reflective people feel grief deeply. Thomas wasn't afraid to be honest about the painful emotions and lingering doubts he felt. This disciple felt that he needed more than just a few words to help him overcome the pain of seeing his Lord cruelly tortured and left to die on a Roman cross. Thomas wanted to see Jesus face to face and touch the resurrected Savior's hands and side. So that's exactly what Jesus asked Thomas to do when He appeared again to the disciples:

> After eight days His disciples were again inside, and Thomas with them. Jesus came, the doors having been shut, and stood in their midst and said, "Peace be with you." Then He said to Thomas, "Reach here with your finger, and see My hands; and reach here your hand and put it into My side; and do not be unbelieving, but believing." Thomas answered and said to Him, "My Lord and my God!" (John 20:26–28)

Take a moment to reread Thomas's extraordinary profession of personal faith in the Messiah, recorded in verse 28. The disciple recognized Jesus's deity as both the risen Lord and the Messiah, sent by the Father above. Thomas's pronouncement indicates that, beyond a shadow of a doubt, he believed that Christ had risen again.

After Thomas's profession of faith, Jesus extended a blessing upon those who had the faith to believe in Him and His resurrection even though they hadn't seen Him physically:

Jesus said to him, "Because you have seen Me, have you believed? Blessed are they who did not see, and yet believed." (20:29)

Jesus willingly offered physical proof to Thomas, doing what was necessary for the disciple to be reassured in his faith. Yet Jesus also reminded him that a special blessing exists for those who trust in God *without* having to see tangible proof on which to base their faith in the here and now.

Have there been times when you wished that God would provide more tangible evidence to dissuade your doubts? If so, describe the circumstances.

_____

_____

_____

_____

What has He provided to boost your faith?

_____

_____

_____

_____

Can you think of any people of the Bible (other than the two mentioned in this chapter) who struggled with doubt? How did God deal with them?

_____

_____

_____

_____

_____

FOUR WAYS WE CAN GROW THROUGH DOUBT

All of us will face moments of doubt and times when we feel that we can't cope with the situations we're encountering. How do we keep growing in the midst of those difficulties?

We grow by risking and failing, not by always playing it safe. You can't afford to live a life of fear. You mustn't always play life safe. Overcoming doubt means beginning to live by faith and not by sight. Walking this new journey has its risks, of course. You cannot see around every bend or anticipate every danger. You will sometimes fail, but failure isn't fatal! Step out in faith.

We grow by releasing and losing things valuable, not by finding security in the temporal. At the heart of this practice is the principle of holding all things loosely. Doubts, fears, and unexpected crises will inevitably enter our lives at some point. But we have the choice to cling to God and His Word for comfort, strength, and an eternal perspective.

We grow by questioning and probing the uncertain, not by mindlessly embracing the orthodox. Don't just blindly swallow someone else's answers. Instead, keep your mind and heart engaged in the pursuit of God's truth. How? By seeking God's wisdom and understanding through daily Bible study, prayer, and interaction with other believers.

We grow by admitting and struggling with our humanity, not by denying our limitations and hiding our fears. God understands when you find yourself cornered by doubt. You are definitely not alone. Most of the great men and women of the

Bible faced doubt in their lives, yet they remain the great heroes and heroines of our faith.

If you find yourself consumed by uncertainty, take a few moments to write down your questions or doubts. Be honest about your fears and feelings.

_____

_____

_____

_____

Confess your doubts to God by writing out a prayer to Him. Ask Him to give you either the grace to accept your uncertainties by faith or the grace to believe and understand what He is doing in your life.

_____

_____

_____

_____

A nonreflective person might ask, "What could be worse than unanswered questions?" A reflective person would reply, "Unquestioned answers!" Jesus promised us that the Father would send the Holy Spirit to give us wisdom and discernment:

> The Helper, the Holy Spirit, whom the Father will send in
> My name, He will teach you all things, and bring to your
> remembrance all that I said to you. Peace I leave with you;
> My peace I give to you; not as the world gives do I give to

you. Do not let your heart be troubled, nor let it be fearful. (John 14:26–27)

Like Thomas, let's be courageous enough to share our true feelings and ask the tough questions. When we establish a relationship with God through Christ, He sends the Holy Spirit to help scatter our doubts and our fears and replace them with the life-changing, supernatural peace that can only come from above.

six

GETTING THROUGH THE
TOUGH STUFF OF DIVORCE

Half of the people in the United States will see their first marriage end in divorce within the first decade of marriage. Sadly, the divorce rate is even higher for second and third marriages. For many of us, the commitment we made to love, honor, and cherish each other "till death do us part" has faded somewhere along the way.

Consider this example from pastor and author Ed Young:

> I witnessed a television wedding recently that was "standard issue" in every way but one. The bride and groom were formally dressed. There were flowers, beautiful music, and family and friends in attendance. Rings were exchanged; vows were spoken—but with one slight variation. The bride and groom promised to "love and cherish,

honor and sustain," but not as long as they both shall live. Oh no. These two promised to keep their vows as long as they both "shall love." Just one letter changes, but oh, what a difference that one letter makes.

What they were saying is this: "Our love is conditional. It is for now, but it may not be for always. We'll have to see how we feel about it down the road. If the day should come when we stop loving each other, the deal is off. The commitment is no longer binding if we don't feel loving toward one another." That's a modern view of marriage—but it is a total misunderstanding of love.[1]

No doubt, you've seen a number of marriages crumble because one or both partners chose to remain committed only "as long as we both shall love." Maybe your own marriage has ended. Perhaps you've suffered through the difficult divorce of your parents, one or more of your children, other family members, or close friends. Or maybe you're going through a particularly rough phase in your current relationship and you're thinking about trying to get out and start over. If you've ever faced one of these situations, or know someone who has, then this chapter is for you!

Let's take some time to discover why God created marriage and how He empowers us to love our spouses for a lifetime. We'll also review Jesus's teaching on divorce and see why it's so important to commit to our spouses forever—not just "as long as we both shall *love*."

WHERE AND HOW MARRIAGE BEGAN

Genesis 1 describes God's glorious creation of the world and its inhabitants. When we read Genesis 1:27, we discover God's crowning creative work, which bore His magnificent image and signature: humanity. Then, Genesis 2 takes us behind the scenes for a closer look at Adam and Eve's creation and blessed union:

> Then the Lord God formed man of dust from the ground, and breathed into his nostrils the breath of life; and man became a living being. . . . Then the Lord God said, "It is not good for the man to be alone; I will make him a helper suitable for him." . . . So the Lord God caused a deep sleep to fall upon the man, and he slept; then He took one of his ribs and closed up the flesh at that place. The Lord God fashioned into a woman the rib which He had taken from the man, and brought her to the man. (2:7, 18, 21–22)

God gave Eve to Adam in the first-ever marriage relationship. Talk about a storybook wedding! We hear no wedding march, no string quartet, no stressed-out wedding planner barking orders at the ushers. We see no bridal gown, no tuxedo, no wedding bands tied to a pillow, no flashes from the photographer's camera. We find only a peaceful garden scene with God, a man, and a woman coming together. A perfect plan, spelled out in simple but profound terms:

> For this reason a man shall leave his father and his mother, and be joined to his wife; and they shall become one flesh.

And the man and his wife were both naked and were not ashamed. (2:24–25)

The brief narrative in Genesis reveals God's original blueprint for marriage, which hasn't changed.

- Marriage is to be a lifelong union between a man and a woman.

- The man and woman are brought together by God Himself.

- God calls the couple to live out their relationship for His glory.

How do these three God-given mandates for marriage differ from today's cultural standards? Give some specific examples.

_____

_____

_____

_____

WHERE MARRIAGE WENT WRONG

What went wrong with this God-ordained, perfect marriage? In a word, *sin*. Most of us know the story. God allowed Adam and Eve the freedom to live in the Garden of Eden and to enjoy its fruits. He gave them only one prohibition: they were not to eat the fruit of the Tree of the Knowledge of Good and Evil. To do so would bring both of them spiritual, as well as physical, death (Genesis 2:17). But Adam and Eve chose to disobey God. Each of them ate that tantalizing forbidden fruit, and by doing so, they set in motion an avalanche of destruction with severe consequences.

Read Genesis 3:7–24. How did the original, perfect marriage partnership between Adam and Eve change after they sinned?

_____

_____

_____

_____

As a result of the snowball effect of sin, what specific struggles do we face in modern marriages that Adam and Eve didn't face in the garden?

_____

_____

_____

_____

JESUS'S INSTRUCTIONS REGARDING DIVORCE

Setting the scene of Adam and Eve's God-ordained partnership helps us to understand why Jesus expressed so much concern about divorce. Even in His day, divorce was rampant among the common people as well as in the religious circles of the Pharisees. In Matthew 19, we see how the religious leaders put Jesus to the test regarding the tough stuff of divorce:

> Some Pharisees came to Jesus, testing Him and asking, "Is it lawful for a man to divorce his wife for any reason at all?" (Matthew 19:3)

God intended for His chosen nation, Israel, to bear witness of Him throughout the world. But, even in the early days, the Jewish people floundered in sin and unbelief. Because the people chose to disobey God by sinning in numerous ways, including intermarrying with people from pagan cultures, Old Testament Law permitted a man to give his wife a certificate of divorce if "some indecency" was found in her (Deuteronomy 24:1–4).

What did the term "some indecency" mean?

> In mainstream Palestinian Judaism, opinion was divided roughly into two opposing camps: both the school of Hillel and the school of Shammai permitted divorce (of the woman by the man: the reverse was not considered) on the grounds of 'erwat dābār ("something indecent," Deut. 24:1), but they disagreed on what "indecent" might include. Shammai and his followers interpreted the expression to refer to gross indecency, though not necessarily adultery; Hillel extended the meaning beyond sin to all kinds of real or imagined offenses, including an improperly cooked meal. The Hillelite R. Akiba permitted divorce in the case of a roving eye for prettier women."[2]

By asking Jesus the question, "Is it lawful for a man to divorce his wife for any reason at all?" the Pharisees tried to draw Him into the Hillel-Shammai controversy. No matter how Christ answered their question, He would make enemies, and the Pharisees hoped they could use His words to trap Him and bring Him down.

However, rather than be pulled into this controversy, Jesus aligned Himself with the prophet Malachi, who recorded God's strong feelings toward divorce: "For I hate divorce" (Malachi 2:16). And just why does God hate divorce so much? Because it goes against His original plan and purposes, and it wrecks lives.

Rather than list all of the negative effects of divorce, however, Jesus reminded the Pharisees of God's perfect design for marriage:

> And He answered and said, "Have you not read that He who created them from the beginning made them male and female, and said, 'For this reason a man shall leave his father and mother and be joined to his wife, and the two shall become one flesh'? So they are no longer two, but one flesh. What therefore God has joined together, let no man separate." (Matthew 19:4–6)

Frustrated, the Pharisees regrouped to think for a few minutes. Then, still determined to draw Jesus into their heated debate, they tried to play off His response by asking Him a tricky question.

> They said to Him, "Why then did Moses command to give her a certificate of divorce and send her away?" He said to them, "Because of your hardness of heart Moses *permitted* you to divorce your wives; but from the beginning it has not been this way. And I say to you, whoever divorces his wife, except for immorality, and marries another woman commits adultery." (Matthew 19:7–9, emphasis added)

Notice something surprising here. Jesus never said that the faithful, offended partner is *commanded* to leave. He never even suggested that he or she *should* leave. He said only that he or she is *permitted* to leave, and even then, only in the case of immorality.

Jesus emphasized that in God's economy, divorce represents the exception and not the rule. Author John R. W. Stott explains that God allows divorce "only [as] a divine concession to human weakness."[3] Divorce was not a part of God's original design. It deeply grieves Him to see His people turning their backs on their sacred marriage vows.

It's important to consider Jesus's words in context. When He spoke of "immorality" in the context of divorce, He was referring to much more than a quick, one-night act of infidelity. Yes, Jesus deeply understood that any infidelity in marriage causes extreme grief, pain, and feelings of betrayal. But He also knew that God's ultimate desire is for the faithful partner to stay in the marriage, allowing the Healer the opportunity to mend and restore the fractured relationship.

Of course, in certain instances, it may be unsafe for one partner and his or her children to remain in a marriage,

GETTING TO THE ROOT

In Matthew 19:9, Matthew uses the Greek term *porneia*, translated "immorality." The English word *pornography* comes from this term. *Porneia* is not limited to adultery, but also includes incest, lesbian sex, homosexual acts, and any *sustained* lifestyle of deviant sexual conduct outside the marriage. By using this word, Jesus referred to a *continued willingness* on the part of one marriage partner to remain sexually unfaithful.

especially in the case of emotional or physical abuse. In this case, separation may be necessary, at least for a time. But, unless it would compromise our physical safety, God's priority for marriage is restoration, not separation.

What do Jesus's words tell us about the sanctity of marriage? What do we learn about God's attitude toward divorce?

_____

_____

_____

_____

_____

No doubt, forgiving an unfaithful spouse and agreeing to help mend the marriage is one of the most difficult things God could ever ask us to do. But those who choose to forgive their unfaithful partner and stay married often say later, "Staying together was the best thing we ever did. I decided to forgive him [or her]. I understood that the acts represented a failure, a breaking of our intimacy. But I've determined that our faith, our marriage, our children, and our future are worth dealing with this and moving on." And they are.

It's troubling to see that Christian couples are as susceptible to divorce as are non-Christians. In spite of the inexhaustible divine resources at our disposal, the odds of a Christian marriage lasting a lifetime are just as low as for unbelievers. Divorce has become an epidemic, and it's wreaking havoc—not just on us, but on our children, including our adult children. Our country's emerging generations are being crippled by this epidemic.

All marriages face rocky times marked by trials, temptations, and disappointments. But we've taken a sacred vow before God, our spouse, and witnesses that we will stay married "as long as we both shall live." God ordained marriage, and only He can provide us with the supernatural power to remain with our spouse through the tough times of life.

Four Essentials for a Godly Marriage

Genesis 1 and 2 reveal that God intends every marriage to possess four essential ingredients: *severance, permanence, unity,* and *intimacy.*

Severance. "A man shall leave his father and his mother." God planned for both the bride and the groom to sever their dependent ties with their original parents or guardians. This ensures that the relationship begins without competing emotions. It also implies a clear dependence on God and interdependence on each other.

Permanence. "And be joined to his wife." The Greek word translated "be joined to" literally means "to bond, to glue." God had permanence in mind. Adam and Eve were to have a lifelong, impenetrable relationship.

Unity. "And they shall become one flesh." The man and the woman were to enjoy different roles and to maintain their unique God-given traits and temperaments. At the same time, God meant for them to experience an incredible oneness, an overarching unity that would prevail.

Intimacy. "And the man and his wife were both naked and were not ashamed." Adam and Eve enjoyed a tender, God-ordained intimacy that was completely untarnished by sin, unfettered by shame, and absent of self-consciousness. The intimate delights of that first husband and wife are beyond our comprehension. Their marriage was perfect—absolutely perfect. Then came Genesis 3.

Sin took its toll on permanence even more than it did on severance, unity, and intimacy. Sin destroyed the marriage bond that had been sealed at God's holy altar. Sin caused a massive blot on the record of human relationships from that day until now, and that blot especially mars the permanence of our marriages.

If you're married, which of the four essentials listed above are easiest for you to maintain? How do you maintain them?

_____

_____

_____

_____

_____

Which essentials are the most difficult for you to maintain, and why?

_____

_____

_____

_____

_____

How do you think your spouse would answer these questions?

_____

_____

_____

_____

_____

TAKING TRUTH TO HEART

Remember the following three thoughts as you consider Christ's teaching on divorce:

The sanctity of marriage necessitates personal commitment. We have no right to end our marriages simply because of difficulties or inconveniences. Believe it or not, no marriage is held together simply by romantic love. We certainly need love, but we also need commitment to add "muscle" to our marriages.

The necessity of commitment is weakened by our sinful nature. In weak moments, we're all tempted to walk out. Sin enters, and with it comes compromise, a softening of our wills, and any number of carnal by-products: abuse, infidelity, selfishness, arguments, grudges, caustic remarks, and sarcasm. All of these weaken our commitment. We need help at this point in order to carry on.

Our sinful nature can be counteracted by Jesus Christ. No matter how desperately dysfunctional your marriage has become, God is the answer. When we have established a relationship with Him through our Lord and Savior, Jesus Christ, we have the strength we need to follow God's perfect design for marriage. We have a model of grace and forgiveness that we can follow when times get tough.

If you're married, rank your current level of commitment on the scale below. In what ways can you adjust your commitment to better reflect God's desires for your marriage?

uncommitted   very strong

1   2   3   4   5

_____

_____

_____

Whom do you know currently dealing with the tough stuff of divorce? How can you use the principles you've learned in this chapter to guide him or her?

_____

_____

_____

Unless you have a strong relationship with God through Christ, a solid marriage is virtually impossible to maintain. If your marriage is already on the rocks, you must not attempt to go through the tough stuff of even contemplating divorce without leaning hard on God (and possibly a Christian counselor or friend). With God as the foundation, no marriage is too far gone. Unless your marriage partner has passed away or remarried (we'll discuss remarriage in the next chapter), there's never a point of no return if you are willing to surrender to Him and allow Him to work His way . . . and in His time.

You may have already been through (or are going through) the tough stuff of divorce. Regardless of the circumstances leading to that decision, God accepts you and loves you. Remember, there's at least one person who understands the hurt you've been through. He knows the sting and shame of rejection, the horror of injustice, and the shock of unfaithfulness. His name is Jesus. He endured the Cross and so much more to save you from your sins and your heartache. Only He can take the shattered pieces of your life and lovingly begin to put them back together again. Take a moment to pray now and ask God to help you (or your loved one) make it through the tough stuff of divorce. He's waiting with open arms!

seven

GETTING THROUGH THE
TOUGH STUFF OF REMARRIAGE

D ivorce is one of the most painful experiences that any of us could face. Yet once a person has experienced divorce, he or she faces another difficult dilemma: whether or not to remarry. The challenges and issues involved with remarriage can present a real obstacle, especially for Christ-followers.

Pastors, scholars, counselors, parents, and friends may offer varying opinions and advice regarding remarriage. Some believe that God approves of remarriage and blesses those who choose to marry again. Others believe that God may *allow* remarriage in certain instances but doesn't necessarily look kindly upon it. Some people feel that no one should remarry except in the case of a spouse's death, while others feel that remarriage should be forbidden, no matter what.

As we move forward in our attempt to gain wisdom regarding remarriage, let's turn to Scripture to see the principles that God lays out for us on the issue.

THREE BIBLICAL CASES FOR REMARRIAGE

A Spouse Chooses a Life of Immorality

The Bible lists three instances in which remarriage after divorce is permissible. The first is when one spouse chooses to pursue a life of immorality. We find this example discussed in Matthew 19, which we also addressed in the previous chapter of this workbook. When the Pharisees tried to set a trap for Jesus by questioning Him about the grounds for divorce, He answered:

> And I say to you, whoever divorces his wife, except for immorality, and marries another woman commits adultery. (Matthew 19:9)

God hates divorce, as He clearly states in Malachi 2:16. But it also grieves Him when He sees the sacred bond of marriage desecrated by a spouse who continually pursues a promiscuous lifestyle and refuses to repent. In situations where one partner is involved in an immoral relationship outside the marriage, God allows the faithful partner the option to divorce the unfaithful partner and remarry.

Read Matthew 19:1–9. Drawing on what you learned in the previous chapter about the word porneia *(immorality) and Jesus's response to the Pharisees' questions, was Jesus saying that any immoral sin was grounds for divorce? How do you know this? How does this affect what Jesus said about remarriage in verse 9?*

_____

_____

_____

_____

_____

An Unbelieving Spouse Deserts a Christian Mate

The second case in which God allows remarriage is when a non-Christian mate deserts a Christian mate. We find this case addressed in 1 Corinthians 7. In the beginning of this chapter, the apostle Paul states that he would prefer all people to remain unmarried, like himself, in order to dedicate their lives fully to Christ. He admits, however, that "each man has his own gift from God, one in this manner, and another in that" (7:7). Those individuals who do not have the gift of celibacy—the God-given ability to remain single and content—are free to pursue a marriage partnership with a member of the opposite sex.

Paul goes on to describe three categories of people and how each group should approach the issue of marriage and remarriage. The first people he addresses are those he refers to as "the unmarried" in verses 8 and 9. This category includes the never-married, widows, and currently unmarried people. Paul says he prefers that they all remain unmarried so they can devote themselves wholeheartedly to Christ. But if they simply cannot remain unmarried and content, they should marry or remarry, whatever the case.

Next, Paul addresses "the married," and to them he issues a challenge to *stay* married. Specifically, he states:

> But to the married I give instructions, not I, but the Lord,
> that the wife should not leave her husband (but if she does

leave, she must remain unmarried, or else be reconciled to her husband), and that the husband should not divorce his wife. (1 Corinthians 7:10–11)

Paul urges those already married to find contentment with their spouse, just as he consistently did throughout his letters to believers. But he also understood the harsh realities of life. At times, an abused or mistreated spouse must flee to preserve his or her own life or to protect his or her children. In desperate situations such as these, separation is permitted for the sake of health and safety. Today, we would counsel both partners in a case like this to seek professional help. To those suffering in difficult situations, Paul offers the parenthetical statement in verse 11, which allows separation for the purpose of later reconciliation.

Next, Paul addresses those who are "unequally yoked" in marriage—believers who are married to unbelievers:

But to the rest I say . . . that if any brother has a wife who is an unbeliever, and she consents to live with him, he must not divorce her. And a woman who has an unbelieving husband, and he consents to live with her, she must not send her husband away. For the unbelieving husband is sanctified through his wife, and the unbelieving wife is sanctified through her believing husband; for otherwise your children are unclean, but now they are holy. Yet if the unbelieving one leaves, let him leave; the brother or the sister is not under bondage in such cases, but God has

called us to peace. For how do you know, O wife, whether
you will save your husband? Or how do you know, O husband, whether you will save your wife? (1 Corinthians
7:12–16)

In this passage, Paul urges us toward permanence where possible, even in a
spiritually unbalanced relationship. The presence of a saved partner in the
home sets the home apart and sanctifies it. The children are under the influence of biblical truth because one parent is a believer and knows the Lord
personally. The Christian's spouse may not care about the things of Christ,
but at least the non-Christian lives in the presence and under the influence of
a godly, loving partner.

Now, let's focus on the words "not under bondage" in verse 15. As you
would imagine, this phrase has stirred up a firestorm of controversy over the
years. In marriage, a man and woman are bound together in love, unity, and
commitment. We find a reference to this idea in 1 Corinthians:

A wife is *bound* as long as her husband lives; but if her husband is dead, she is free to be married to whom she wish-
es, only in the Lord. (1 Corinthians 7:39, emphasis added)

This verse clarifies that in the case of the death of one spouse, the other
spouse is released from his or her marriage bond and is free to remarry. In
addition, a Christian partner released from the marriage due to desertion by
an unbeliever may also remarry. Perhaps you're a wife whose unsaved husband
has left, slamming the door of reconciliation forever shut behind him. Or

maybe you're a husband whose former wife has remarried, and therefore you know the bond between the two of you is broken. According to God's Word, you are now free to remarry if you choose.

According to 1 Corinthians 7:7–16, which of the three categories do you fall into—the unmarried, the married, or the unequally yoked? In light of your own situation, what does Paul advocate? What does he permit?

_____

_____

_____

_____

What is the difference between what Paul recommends and what he allows? Why do you think he makes this distinction?

_____

_____

_____

_____

A Marriage Fails Prior to Salvation

The third biblical case for remarriage occurs when a person's prior marriage failed before he or she became a believer. This case is based on two verses from 2 Corinthians 5:

> Therefore from now on we recognize no one according to
> the flesh; even though we have known Christ according to

the flesh, yet now we know Him in this way no longer. Therefore if anyone is in Christ, *he is a new creature;* the old things passed away; behold, new things have come. (2 Corinthians 5:16–17, emphasis added)

GETTING TO THE ROOT

The Greek term *kainos* in verse 17 means "new" or "fresh."[1] This word doesn't mean new with regard to time, but in terms of form and substance. When an individual moves from death to life through faith in Jesus Christ, he or she becomes a *kainos* creation. He or she is born again. Everything is fresh and new. Isn't that magnificent? All his or her transgressions are forgiven and erased.

If you're a Christian, do you remember what life was like when you were lost? Remember what a different person you were then? These verses provide a good reminder of the radical change that has occurred in your life between then and now. When you chose to follow Christ, you received a fresh start—immediately! The old Law passed away, and you're now living in grace. You're a new creation! According to Psalm 103:12, "As far as the east is from the west, so far has He removed our transgressions from us." If you experienced the pain of a failed marriage before you became a Christian, you're now free to pursue remarriage—but this time, be sure to choose a godly partner.

Have you, a friend, or a family member had a marriage fail prior to becoming a believer?
If so, why would 2 Corinthians 5:17 be especially encouraging to you or that person?

_____

_____

_____

_____

_____

_____

TAKING TRUTH TO HEART

Certain species of animals—some ducks, for instance—mate for life. In fact, scientific studies have documented that even in the event of the death of a mate, ducks often remain perfectly faithful, choosing to die beside their mate rather than leave their lifelong partner.

Marriage was meant to be like that: not an easy street, but a partnership that stands the test of time, even on an exhilarating, wild, and dangerous frontier. In his book *The Mystery of Marriage,* Mike Mason writes:

> Everywhere else, throughout society, there are fences, walls, burglar alarms, unlisted numbers, the most elaborate precautions for keeping people at a safe distance. But in marriage all of that is reversed. In marriage the walls are down, and not only do the man and woman live under the same roof, but they sleep under the same covers. Their lives are wide open, and as each studies the life

of the other and attempts to make some response to it, there are no set procedures to follow, no formalities to stand on. A man and a woman face each other across the breakfast table, and somehow through a haze of crumbs and curlers and mortgage payments they must encounter one another. That is the whole purpose and mandate of marriage. All sorts of other purposes have been dreamed up and millions of excuses invented for avoiding this central and indispensable task. But the fact is that marriage is grounded in nothing else but the pure wild grappling of soul with soul, no holds barred. There is no rule book for this, no law to invoke except the law of love.

So while marriage may present the appearance of being a highly structured, formalized, and tradition-bound institution, in fact it is the most free and raw and unpredictable of all human associations. It is the outer space of society, the wild frontier.[2]

And so it should be. Husbands and wives were meant to fly free—free alongside each other. As partners bound together for life, lovers who know the joys and ecstasies of intimacy, and friends willing to stay when the other falls, husbands and wives were meant to stay to the very end with the one they have chosen to love.

What lessons can we learn from ducks' faithfulness to their mates?

_____

_____

_____

_____

What characteristics of marriage do you think make it "the outer space of society, the wild frontier"? Why?

_____

_____

_____

_____

FOUR EXHORTATIONS FOR ALL WHO ARE MARRIED— OR WHO HOPE TO BE SOMEDAY

Married couples can easily slip into naive bliss, ignorant of the inevitable challenges ahead. Because this is true, we'll close this chapter by offering four exhortations to remember in order to protect you and your marriage—or future marriage—from slow erosion that could result in a painful demise.

To the unmarried: *Be patient!* Some will remain wonderfully content as a single adult all their lives, while others pray, ache, and long for a marriage partner. Don't allow the desire for a mate to rush you into making a commitment you could live to regret. Take the time to choose a mate prayerfully and wisely. Believe it or not, there *is* something worse than not having a marriage partner— having the wrong one! So be patient and wait on God's perfect timing.

To the married: *Be content!* God is sovereign. He is at work, and He'll be faithful to you, regardless of your situation. Keep reality uppermost in your mind. You may enjoy watching couples matched on the latest reality TV show, but you must realize that there's nothing *real* about reality TV. Don't rely on the latest movies or television shows to present an accurate view of married life—ever! Real marriage is different from what you see on TV. Contentment comes as God changes *you* and your attitudes. Don't concentrate on simply trying to change your spouse to match Hollywood's unrealistic expectations.

To those married people who are struggling and have biblical grounds for ending your marriage: *Be careful!* You and your spouse are the most vulnerable ducks on the pond. You may be so starved for a loving, godly relationship that you're vulnerable to danger, teetering on the brink of disaster. Proceed with care. Guard yourself against a fall. Invest as much as you can into keeping your marriage together. Find a trusted pastor, counselor, or Christian friend and seek his or her counsel regarding the marital problems that you're facing.

To the remarried: *Be grateful and understanding!* Even if you have biblical grounds for divorce and remarriage, you may not find complete acceptance everywhere you go. Not every church or organization will throw its arms around you and heap praise on you for the choices you've made. Don't hold your breath waiting for that to happen. Instead, remain grateful to the Lord for His provision and His matchless grace. Try your best to show understanding and love, even toward those who don't agree with your choices. As you do so, God will use you to have a ministry in the lives of others that you may never have dreamed possible.

What would you say are the most difficult challenges people face in marriage?

_____

_____

_____

_____

What are the benefits of sticking with marriage, despite the challenges? List as many as you can think of.

_____

_____

_____

_____

If you're married and you're currently struggling with a particular issue in your marriage, what do you think God would say to you right now about the issue? What steps might you take to change your attitudes and actions about it?

_____

_____

_____

_____

If you're married, list three ways you can demonstrate your love and commitment to your partner today.

_____

_____

_____

_____

To you who are remarried, enjoy your new relationship. This is the marriage you want to last a lifetime! Cultivate it. Deepen your love. Remember your sacred vows. Enjoy your new life, but also keep in mind the important lessons you've learned from your past experiences. You can be sure that, somewhere on your life's journey, God will use those lessons to make an impact in the lives of others who are struggling with the tough stuff of divorce and remarriage.

eight

GETTING THROUGH THE
TOUGH STUFF OF CONFRONTATION

We've all heard the saying "Experience is the best teacher." And in most cases, it's true. We certainly learn by doing. But, as any parent or instructor would agree, we could add a word to this maxim to make it even more accurate: Guided experience is the best teacher.

What's the difference between experience and guided experience? Guided experience implies that we're not learning in isolation; we're being observed, steered, coached, coaxed, and corrected by someone else. This adds a crucial and often uncomfortable element to the process: confrontation. Confrontation occurs when a piano teacher reminds her student to use the proper technique. It occurs when a senior pilot corrects the calculations of a young pilot in training. Confrontation helps us learn the right way to do things.

Sadly, we usually avoid confrontation because the thought of it carries such a negative connotation. We've all been offended by people who rudely *affronted* us rather than lovingly *confronting* us. There's a world of difference between the two!

For us to get through the tough stuff of confrontation, we must gain a solid understanding of God's perspective on the process. Let's see what His Word has to say about the issue.

Gaining an Understanding of Biblical Confrontation

GETTING TO THE ROOT

The Hebrew word *qadam*, translated "confront," means "to come or be in front, to meet."[1] In Greek, the word *ephistemi*, ("confronted") appears only in Luke 20:1 and means "to set upon, set up, to stand upon, be present."[2]

The word *confront* appears only a few times in the Bible, yet the concept runs like a thread through the fabric of biblical history.

At least five synonyms for *confrontation* appear in Scripture. Let's examine each one now so we can learn when, why, and how to biblically confront others.

Reproof

The first synonym is *reproof.* No one enjoys being reproved—or reproving others, for that matter. But at times it may be necessary, whether we like it or not. Often reproof serves to uncover blind spots in our character and to help us grow. This is especially true when the reproof comes from God or from a trusted friend who has our best interests at heart. In fact, Proverbs teaches us:

> He is on the path of life who heeds instruction,
> But he who ignores reproof goes astray. (Proverbs 10:17)

> Whoever loves discipline loves knowledge,
> But he who hates reproof is stupid. (Proverbs 12:1)

> Poverty and shame will come to him who neglects discipline,
> But he who regards reproof will be honored. (Proverbs 13:18)

Rebuke

Another synonym, *rebuke*, has more of a stern connotation than *reproof*, but it still carries the sense of guided confrontation.

> A rebuke goes deeper into one who has understanding
> Than a hundred blows into a fool. (Proverbs 17:10)

You can try to correct a fool day after day, and you'll make little progress. But when you correct a godly person who has a teachable spirit, your rebuke should be sufficient to cause that person to change his or her behavior or attitude.

Wound

Confrontation can be a "wounding" experience, but if the confronter is a friend who truly loves us, the benefits of his or her reproof are real and lasting.

> Faithful are the wounds of a friend,
> But deceitful are the kisses of an enemy. (Proverbs 27:6)

Few people have earned the right to "wound" us—only close, trustworthy friends. Yet some people (especially fellow Christians!) see themselves as having the "spiritual gift" of confrontation. They may even use Scripture to support their damaging behavior. But they'll find that people are much more open to being confronted by someone who truly loves and cares about them. When you consider confronting another person, check your motives and your relationship. Have you earned the right?

Correct

A fourth synonym is *correct*, which suggests that confrontation is designed to improve one's character. In the original language, this term carries the idea of rescuing a person from the wrong path and placing him or her on the correct one.

> Correct your son, and he will give you comfort;
> He will also delight your soul. (Proverbs 29:17)

Discipline

Scripture often uses the word *discipline* as a synonym for *confrontation*. For a closer look at this word, turn to the book of Hebrews.

> All discipline for the moment seems not to be joyful, but sorrowful; yet to those who have been trained by it, afterwards it yields the peaceful fruit of righteousness. (Hebrews 12:11)

Reprove. Rebuke. Wound. Correct. Discipline. These five terms and their nuances of meaning offer us a composite picture of what godly confrontation should be:

> *Confrontation is speaking the truth in a personal,*
> *face-to-face encounter with someone we love regarding an issue*
> *that needs attention or correction.*

Biblical confrontation is a difficult, yet necessary art that we must learn. We may find it easy to affront a person, but to confront a person in a biblical way, with the goals of maturity and restoration in mind, requires an extraordinary outpouring of God's grace.

Describe a time when someone in your life confronted you. Which of the methods we've described in this chapter was used?

_____

_____

_____

_____

What did the confronter say to you, and how did you respond?

_____

_____

_____

_____

Name a time when you have confronted someone else. Which method or methods did you use?

_____

_____

_____

_____

_____

What was the outcome of the confrontation?

_____

_____

_____

_____

Four Guidelines for Confrontation

Getting through the tough stuff of confrontation requires some deliberate thinking. Thankfully, Scripture offers us four powerful guiding principles that help us distill confrontation into terms we can apply.

State the issue tactfully and directly. When you choose to confront a person in love, do so in private, and try your best to communicate your thoughts clearly. You can deliver your message firmly, yet still have a gracious attitude toward the person you're confronting.

Provide examples without exaggeration or excess emotion. When you choose to confront someone, point out those things that concern you, and then state why. Provide specific examples, but keep your emotions in check. Allow enough time between the offense and the confrontation for prayerful diffusing of your anger and hurt.

Suggest a plan of action. Don't leave the individual without offering clear direction for how to improve. After you've gently approached the person, asked to pray with him or her if possible, identified the problem, and stated why it bothers you, calmly suggest ways that the problem can be corrected.

Show compassion and understanding. This one is essential throughout the process. Don't miss this part! If you do, you will find yourself accusing others rather than confronting them. Compassion, care, understanding, and love are essential for a successful confrontation.

When faced with the need to confront people about their behavior or attitude, do you tend to shrink from it? What about when you're the one being confronted—do you tend to fight or flee? Why do you think this is the case?

Which of the four guidelines just discussed do you find the most difficult to keep in mind and follow when confrontation arises? How can you make sure that you follow this guideline and also express love the next time you have to confront?

These principles are more easily understood when we see them in action, so let's study a biblical example. The apostle Peter routinely needed Christ's firm confrontation. Jesus provided the instruction Peter needed through a series of interventions that helped develop in him a rugged, resilient faith.

JESUS AND PETER: BIBLICAL CONFRONTATION IN ACTION

As the shadow of the cross loomed on the horizon of Jesus's life, His need to confront the apostles increased and intensified. Three passages portray His encounters with Peter, a man whom He deeply loved and who repeatedly expressed remarkable devotion to his Master. In each one, Jesus skillfully and lovingly shapes Peter's character. From these scenes, we can learn when, why, and how to confront.

When to Confront

The first scene takes place as Jesus informs the disciples of His approaching death.

> From that time Jesus began to show His disciples that He
> must go to Jerusalem, and suffer many things from the eld-
> ers and chief priests and scribes, and be killed, and be
> raised up on the third day. (Matthew 16:21)

The disciples were waiting for Jesus to establish His earthly kingdom—one that would deliver them from the power and oppression of Gentile rule. The idea of a suffering Messiah never penetrated. Rather than embracing such a concept, they wanted to protect Him from it.

> Peter took Him aside began to rebuke Him, saying, "God
> forbid it, Lord! This shall never happen to You." (Matthew
> 16:22)

The zealous disciple thought he had Jesus's best interest at heart, but actually, he had the wrong perspective and wound up with his foot in his mouth. Jesus wasted no time in confronting Peter about this misunderstanding.

> But He turned and said to Peter, "Get behind Me, Satan!
> You are a stumbling block to Me; for you are not setting
> your mind on God's interests, but man's." (Matthew 16:23)

No one loved Peter more than the Savior. And no one ever saw more poten-
tial in Peter than Jesus. That's why He cared enough to confront him.
From this poignant scene, we find two answers to the question of when to

confront. First, we confront people when their actions become stumbling blocks to us or others or, certainly, to the gospel. And second, we confront when people have their minds set on their own interests rather than God's.

Why to Confront

The second scene is of even greater magnitude than the first because it takes us closer to the Cross. In the privacy of the Upper Room, Jesus had just finished a dramatic lesson on what it meant to be a servant, which He illustrated by washing the disciples' feet. What He said next must have sent more shock waves through the room, as He again directed His words to Peter:

> Simon, Simon, behold, Satan has demanded permission to sift you like wheat; but I have prayed for you; that your faith may not fail; and you, when once you have turned again, strengthen your brothers. (Luke 22:31–32)

Can you imagine being singled out in front of your peers and being told that Satan has a plan just for you? Literally, Jesus said, "Satan has begged earnestly for you." Do you think Satan still does this? Absolutely. But, thankfully, the Savior still prays for our preservation and strength (see John 17:15; 1 John 2:1).

We would be wise to remember this scene when tempted to go it alone apart from the protection of Christ. Satan would like nothing better than for us to develop overinflated self-confidence. He rejoices when he sees us independently strutting our stuff. That's when we're most vulnerable, and that's the very trap into which Peter had fallen. We recognize Peter's vulnerability when we read his response to Jesus's words:

> Lord, with You I am ready to go both to prison and to death! (Luke 22:33)

In other words, "Lord, bring it on! I can handle anything—not just a dark, filthy prison cell, but even death itself. I'm Your man." Not surprisingly, Jesus confronted Peter's pious braggadocio:

> I say to you, Peter, the rooster will not crow today until you have denied three times that you know Me. (Luke 22:34)

This scene helps us understand why we confront. By confronting, we strengthen areas of vulnerability. We also confront to soften overconfidence and to warn of blind spots. Confronting those we love helps protect them from Satan's sinister assaults and from their own self-destructive ways.

How to Confront

The final scene opens in the early morning hours on the day of Christ's death. An angry mob emerged from the darkness, their torches flickering in the shadows of the olive trees. Judas, the traitor, led the posse (Luke 22:47–48). Despite their terror, the disciples standing with Jesus bravely tried to rally in His defense:

> When those who were around Him saw what was going to
> happen, they said, "Lord, shall we strike with the sword?"
> And one of them struck the slave of the high priest and cut
> off his right ear. (Luke 22:49–50)

Peter, the impetuous one, had struck again (John 18:10)! But Jesus immediately took control of the situation, confronting him.

> But Jesus answered and said, "Stop! No more of this." And
> He touched [the slave's] ear and healed him. (Luke 22:51)

After addressing Peter, Jesus turned His attention to the venomous band of religious leaders standing ready to apprehend Him, saying:

> Have you come out with swords and clubs as you would
> against a robber? While I was with you daily in the temple,
> you did not lay hands on Me; but this hour and the power
> of darkness are yours. (Luke 22:52–53)

Jesus did not lash out or cower in fear. He addressed the issue head on. But His accusers ignored Jesus's straightforward question, arrested Him, and dragged Him to the home of the high priest. Not too far behind lurked a frightened Peter—once overconfident, now fearing for his life. Slinking through the shadows, the stalwart fisherman did what he swore he'd never do. When pressed about his own identity, he denied knowing his Lord (Luke 22:54–60). Not once. Not twice. But three separate times, exactly as Jesus had predicted just a few hours earlier.

Immediately after his third denial, Peter heard the rooster crow. At once, he caught the gaze of the Master whom he had denied.

> The Lord turned and looked at Peter. And Peter remem-
> bered the word of the Lord, how He had told Him, "Before
> the rooster crows today, you will deny Me three times."
> And he went out and wept bitterly. (Luke 22:61–62)

Looking back over these remarkable scenes, we discover four techniques of confrontation Jesus used to correct Peter and His accusers. These people-affirming, God-honoring methods are available to us as well.

- *An abrupt, passionate command*—"Stop! No more of this" (Luke 22:51).

- *A thought-provoking question*—"Have you come out with swords and clubs as you would against a robber?" (22:52).

- *A well-worded analytical statement*—"While I was with you daily in the temple, you did not lay hands on Me; but this hour and the power of darkness are yours" (22:53).

- *A mere glance*—"The Lord turned and looked at Peter. And Peter remem-bered the word of the Lord" (22:61). A probing, intense glance without a word can speak volumes.

How do you think you would have felt if you had been in Peter's shoes and heard the words "Get behind Me, Satan"?

_____

_____

_____

_____

_____

What truths did Jesus illustrate to Peter by confronting him? What did Peter learn about himself through the confrontation and his later actions?

_____

_____

_____

_____

_____

What new insights have you gleaned by studying Peter's and Jesus's interaction in these passages? How can you apply these insights to your own relationships?

_____

_____

_____

_____

TAKING TRUTH TO HEART

From Jesus's example, we can glean three essentials for biblical confrontation.

Be sure. Be sure you have a good reason to confront another individual before you do so. Confrontations should be rare events in your life, not frequent ones. You shouldn't relish these experiences! If you find that you do, be concerned enough to stop and examine your motives.

Be specific. Be specific about the purpose of the confrontation. Being vague can lead to a negative outcome. Make certain you know the real reason for the confrontation, and then make that reason clear to the person you confront. If possible, support your purpose with Scripture.

Be sensitive. An extended season of soul searching and prayer must precede any face-to-face confrontation. Without this discipline of reflection, you're setting yourself up for an enemy assault. Pay attention to your timing and choose your words carefully.

Confrontation is some of the toughest stuff in life, especially when it means challenging a person you really love. But if you care for that person dearly, as Christ loved Peter, you won't hold back. You'll care enough to confront.

nine

GETTING THROUGH THE
TOUGH STUFF OF PAIN

Y ou may know Him as the Lord of Hosts. The Prince of Peace. The Chief
Shepherd. The Bright and Morning Star. The Lion of the Tribe of Judah. The
Lamb of God. The Anointed of God. The Wonderful Counselor. And we could
go on and on! All of these kingly, majestic, victorious names seem perfectly
appropriate for Jesus, the Son of God.

Now, what about "Man of Sorrows"? That doesn't sound quite so wonderful, does it? But to those of us facing the tough stuff of pain, knowing that
Jesus was a man of sorrows helps us to trust Him with our own suffering.

Seven centuries before Jesus's birth, the prophet Isaiah wrote one of the
most powerful chapters in the Old Testament regarding the coming Messiah.

> He was despised and forsaken of men,
> A man of sorrows and acquainted with grief;

And like one from whom men hide their face

He was despised, and we did not esteem Him.

(Isaiah 53:3)

Take a few minutes to read the names of Jesus in Isaiah 9:6, 44:6, and 61:1; John 1:29; 1 Peter 5:4; Revelation 5:5, and 22:16. Which of the names of Jesus tend to resonate with you the most? Why do you think this is the case?

_____

_____

_____

_____

What do you think of when you hear the name "Man of Sorrows"? In what ways does Jesus fit this description?

_____

_____

_____

GETTING TO THE ROOT

In Hebrew, the root of the word translated "sorrows" is *makob*, which means "pain, sorrow, sufferings."[1] As a "Man of Sorrows," Jesus was literally a man of pain and suffering.

As we read on from verses 4 through 12, Isaiah catalogs more of Christ's sufferings:

- Bore our griefs and carried our sorrows (Isaiah 53:4)

- Stricken, smitten of God, and afflicted (53:4)

- Pierced, crushed, chastened, and scourged (53:5)

- Bore the iniquity of us all (53:6)

- Oppressed, afflicted, like a lamb led to slaughter (53:7)

- Silent before His accusers (53:7)

- Oppressed and judged (53:8)

- Cut off from the land of the living (53:8)

- Assigned a grave with wicked men (53:9)

- Crushed and put to grief (53:10)

- Anguished in His soul (53:11)

- Poured out to death (53:12)

- Numbered with the transgressors (53:12)

Isaiah predicted that all of these painful things would come to pass, and we find in the four Gospels that in the events leading to His death, Christ fulfilled every one of these prophecies. Each item in this list carries enough pain of its own, and the thought of bearing all these horrors at one time is

TAKING TRUTH TO HEART

From the moment we're born until the second we die, pain seldom leaves us, and we never stop trying to lessen it (or trying to get rid of it for good). But, as we've all discovered, pain can teach us important lessons, and it has some redeeming qualities that can help shape our lives.

In his book *Where Is God When It Hurts?* Philip Yancey writes:

> I have never read a poem extolling the virtues of pain, nor seen a statue erected in its honor, nor heard a hymn dedicated to it. Pain is usually defined as "unpleasantness."
>
> Christians don't really know how to interpret pain. If you pinned them up against the wall, in a dark, secret moment, many Christians would probably admit that pain was God's one mistake. He really should have worked a little harder and invented a better way of coping with the world's dangers.
>
> I am convinced that pain gets a bad press. Perhaps we should see statues, hymns, and poems to pain. Why do I think that? Because up close, and under a microscope, the pain network is seen in an entirely different light. It is perhaps the paragon of creative genius.[2]

absolutely beyond comprehension. In the truest sense of the word, Jesus became the ultimate Man of Sorrows, intimately acquainted with grief and pain.

According to Yancey, how do we tend to think of pain in our lives? Do you agree with his assessment?

_____

_____

_____

_____

_____

_____

How can God use our pain to create greater maturity and positive results in our lives? List an example of this from your own experience.

_____

_____

_____

_____

_____

_____

FOUR TYPES OF PAIN THAT CHRIST EXPERIENCED

The pain Jesus experienced on earth can be categorized into four types: relational pain, internal pain, physical pain, and the ultimate pain—the suffering Jesus endured when our sin separated Him from the Father.

Relational Pain

According to Matthew 26:30, Jesus and His disciples ended the Last Supper by singing a hymn. The Twelve, still confused by Jesus's teaching about the betrayal and crucifixion that lay ahead, had no clue about what was going to happen. But Jesus knew. And He also knew, as they headed toward the Garden of Gethsemane, that if ever He needed the support of His close friends, it was now.

> Then Jesus came with them to a place called Gethsemane, and said to His disciples, "Sit here while I go over there and pray." And He took with Him Peter and the two sons of Zebedee, and began to be grieved and distressed. Then He said to them, "My soul is deeply grieved, to the point of death; remain here and keep watch with Me." (Matthew 26:36–38)

The pressure of His grief about the coming events was almost unbearable, so He sought the comfort of His most intimate friends. He took them with Him to the Garden of Gethsemane to pray.

> And He went a little beyond them, and fell on His face and prayed, saying, "My Father, if it is possible, let this cup pass from Me; yet not as I will, but as You will." (Matthew 26:39)

How deep was His pain? Deep enough for Jesus to plead for a way out—any other path than the one that led to the cross. He even felt such great physiological pressure that the capillaries near the surface of His skin burst, causing blood mixed with sweat to flow from His body like the fluid oozing from a wound (see Luke 22:44). Jesus endured extreme physical, mental, emotional, and spiritual anguish in the garden.

Distraught, Jesus removed Himself from His grief momentarily to be encouraged and strengthened by His friends. But just when He needed them most, they failed Him:

> And He came to the disciples and found them sleeping, and said to Peter, "So, you men could not keep watch with Me for one hour? Keep watching and praying that you may not enter into temptation; the spirit is willing, but the flesh is weak." He went away again a second time and prayed, saying, "My Father, if this cannot pass away unless I drink it, Your will be done." Again He came and found them sleeping, for their eyes were heavy. And He left them again, and went away and prayed a third time, saying the same thing once more. (Matthew 26:40–44)

Three times, Jesus left His anguished prayer sessions to seek relief and encouragement from His friends. And three times, they failed Him. Every time He approached them, He found them sleeping. Not one kept his eyes open. Not one stayed by His side. Not one comforted Him. Not one prayed for Him. Sorrow was Jesus's only companion.

Internal Pain

Jesus had known His whole life that this horrible hour would come, but knowing that didn't change His feelings. As He faced the excruciating reality of the cross, He experienced such emotional agony that He fell on His face and earnestly prayed three times for God to let the cup of suffering pass from Him. If there had been any other way, He would have embraced it. His grief in the garden was raw—the thought of experiencing the brunt of God's wrath for our sins must have horrified Him. To know that the Father would have to look away when He bore our sin on the cross must have been almost more than Jesus could bear. The suffering of that hour brought internal pain beyond any that we have ever known.

Physical Pain

Those who have seen the film *The Passion of the Christ* have seen a graphic illustration of the physical pain Christ endured on His way to Calvary. Matthew 26–27 provides an overview of the physical brutalities that Christ experienced:

- Seized and treated harshly like a common criminal (26:57)

- Spit on, slapped, and beaten (26:67)

- Bound and scourged (27:2, 26)

- Spit upon again and beaten with a reed (27:30)

• Mocked (27:31)

• Crucified (27:35)

Imagine the horror of having iron spikes pounded into your hands and into your feet. Or the excruciating humiliation of being hung naked and bleeding in front of the gawking masses. It must have been a horrible event to witness. But enduring it would have been unimaginable.

Jesus's body had been so mutilated that He didn't even look human. Still, there was a pain more severe than that which He felt physically. But, because of Christ's sacrifice, it's a pain you and I will never know.

The Ultimate Pain—Separation from God

Although Christ's relational, internal, and physical pain were horribly intense, the pain of being separated from His Father goes far beyond our ability to imagine.

> Now from the sixth hour darkness fell upon all the land until the ninth hour. About the ninth hour Jesus cried out with a loud voice, saying, "Eli, Eli, lama sabachthani?" that is, "My God, My God, why have You forsaken Me?" (Matthew 27:45–46)

For the first and only time, God turned His back on His Son. At that moment, Christ bore the full weight of our sin. This explains why the Father could not look on Him—because of the offense that our iniquities represented to a holy God. Christ experienced the ultimate pain, which was separation from God the Father. In absolute loneliness and agony, Jesus screamed, "Why have You forsaken Me?" But He already knew the answer: because a holy God could not look on sin.

Why was separation from God the ultimate pain for Jesus?

_____

_____

_____

_____

Spend a few minutes in prayer now, thanking God for sending Jesus to endure such pain and suffering on your behalf. You may use these lines to record your prayer or additional thoughts.

_____

_____

_____

_____

_____

_____

HOPE AND HELP FROM THE SAVIOR

Do you have a lingering scar on your heart that won't heal? Look at His hands, His feet, and His side. Feeling humiliated and alone? He knows what that feels like. Are you so confused by your circumstances that you're tempted to bargain with God for relief? No need. Without one word from your lips, He understands. He identifies with you in your pain.

What scars or painful events are you facing in your life right now?

_____

_____

_____

_____

Does the knowledge that Jesus has "been there" give you encouragement and hope? How does it comfort you to know that He has been through similar painful trials?

_____

_____

_____

_____

Perhaps your lifelong mate has gone to be with the Lord and you face an uncertain and lonely future. Perhaps your husband or your wife just walked out for good, rejecting you and choosing someone else. Or you may have had a falling out with a child, parent, or close friend. Relationally, you need somebody. Internally, you're in anguish. Physically, you've reached your threshold of pain.

You may be full of grief and living with deep emotional scars as a result of being abused. You may suffer from such a shameful addiction that you fear rejection by anyone who might discover your secret. Maybe the pain of your shame grips your soul and ambushes your thoughts. Perhaps you feel helpless, enraged, confused, disappointed, depressed, misunderstood, or humiliated.

Ultimately, you may feel like asking the same question that Jesus did: "God, why have You forsaken me?" But His answer is, "I haven't forsaken you. I've been here all the time! You may have to go through pain for a while, but My purposes will soon be clear to you. I'll get you through it. You can depend on Me." You have hope and help with the Savior by your side.

Four Truths That Help Us Cope

Let's close this chapter with four truths that will provide us with comfort and hope as we walk with Christ through the tough stuff of our pain.

Relationally, no one stays closer than Christ. Christ is better than the most faithful husband, more understanding than the most comforting wife, more reliable than the best of friends. No one stays closer than Christ. There is no friend more caring. No person more unconditionally accessible. There is no one more available or more interested whom you can talk to in the middle of the night or at any moment simply by calling out in prayer. He has promised never to leave you. He will not walk out on you. No one stays closer than Christ.

Internally, no one heals deeper than Christ. You say, "I cannot get over this grief." Yes, you can, but not on your own. That's where Christ is the Master Comforter. Remember, He is intimately "acquainted with grief." He understands what we have to lose. He lost everything for you. He knows what it feels like to suffer in silence, to bear the brunt of unfair criticism, to feel helpless when no one understands, to feel utterly alone when no one is left in your corner. No one heals more deeply than Christ.

Physically, no one comforts better than Christ. In the midst of your deepest physical pain, His hand brings comfort and strength. He may choose to restore your physical health, but frankly, He may not. Regardless, His grace is abundantly sufficient for you. His hand is on your life at the time of your affliction, and it's better than the hand of any friend, partner, parent, or child. When He touches our lives, He brings great compassion and lasting relief. No one comforts better than Christ.

Ultimately, no one sees the benefits of our pain more clearly than Christ. He sees through the winding tunnel of your darkness all the way to the end. You see only the thick, unrelenting darkness. But He sees beyond that into the shining light of eternity. Maturity, growth, stability, wisdom, and, ultimately, the crown of life await the one who trusts His unseen hand. No one sees the benefits of our pain more clearly than Christ.

Which of these four truths resonates with you the most? How can you apply it to the pain that you may be facing right now?

_____

_____

_____

_____

_____

Whatever you're struggling with today, please believe that your pain is no mistake. It's not an accident or a surprise. In fact, your suffering may be precisely what Christ will use to bring you to your knees, to draw you back into His arms so that you can rest in Him and discover His peace.

"Man of Sorrows." The name resonates deeply within us, illustrating exactly what it means for Jesus to be both fully God and fully man. The Man of Sorrows whom we worship is not only the Bright Morning Star (Revelation 22:16), but the holy Lamb of God who died to take away the sins of the world.

With this name, Jesus assures us, "I've been there. I know what it's like to feel pain." He conquered pain so that we can get through the tough stuff with confidence and live abundantly through Him.

ten

GETTING THROUGH THE
TOUGH STUFF OF PREJUDICE

Each of us has seen prejudice rear its ugly head at some point in our lives. And not only have we suffered from those who held prejudices against us, but we've also stereotyped and misjudged others.

Take a minute to think about it. Rich against poor. Educated against uneducated. Palestinian against Jew. Muslim against Christian. Liberal against conservative. White against black. Men against women. On and on prejudice goes, infiltrating every race and culture.

All of us harbor some sort of prejudice against certain people or groups. Some of these prejudices feed themselves in the secret hollows of our souls, but others blatantly show up in our words, attitudes, and actions. Often these attitudes run so deep within our hearts that we become extremely uncomfortable labeling them as "prejudices." But they are! Let's examine what prejudice is and how we can overcome it with God's help.

Defining Prejudice

Webster defines prejudice as a: "preconceived judgment or opinion; an adverse opinion or leaning formed without just grounds or before sufficient knowledge; . . . an irrational attitude of hostility directed against an individual, a group, a race, or their supposed characteristics."[1]

Jesus made it painfully clear that prejudice is a heart problem:

> For from within, out of the heart of men, proceed the evil
> thoughts, fornications, thefts, murders, adulteries, deeds
> of coveting and wickedness, as well as deceit, sensuality,
> envy, slander, pride and foolishness. All these evil things
> proceed from within and defile the man. (Mark 7:21–23)

We don't see the word *prejudice* included in this list, yet the wrong attitudes it represents are part of such phrases as "evil thoughts" and "pride and foolishness." Prejudice begins as a negative thought that escalates into distorted, critical attitudes and cruel words. Such attitudes and words fester until they manifest themselves as acts of verbal assault or physical aggression.

How do you think God feels about prejudice, according to Mark 7:21–23 and James 2:2–4?

_____

_____

_____

_____

_____

GETTING TO THE ROOT

Although the word *prejudice* doesn't appear in the Bible, the word *krinō* ("to judge") is often used with the same connotation.[2]

> For if a man comes into your assembly with a gold ring and dressed in fine clothes, and there also comes in a poor man in dirty clothes, and you pay special attention to the one who is wearing the fine clothes, and say, "You sit here in a good place," and you say to the poor man, "You stand over there, or sit down by my footstool," have you not made distinctions among yourselves, and become *judges* with evil motives? (James 2:2–4, emphasis added)

Have you ever been a victim of someone's prejudice? If so, describe the circumstances. How did you feel, and how did you respond?

_____

_____

_____

_____

Why did you choose this particular response? If you had the situation to do over again, would you respond differently?

_____

_____

_____

_____

PREJUDICE IN JESUS'S DAY

Prejudice frequently reared its ugly head in Jesus's day. And because He's experienced it in all its fury, we need Him by our side as we face the tough stuff of prejudice.

Cultural Prejudice

In the first century, the Holy Land was only one hundred and twenty miles long. Galilee sat in the northernmost territory. Located in the southern region was Judea. Across the central section stretched the territory of Samaria. The Jewish people hated the Samaritans so much that they refused to travel through Samaritan country.

Why would the Jews do this? Because the Samaritans were considered "impure Jews" who had intermarried with pagan cultures. One author describes them as "a mixed race with a pagan core."[3] The Jewish people considered it such a gross insult to be contaminated by Samaritan dust that they would rather add twice as many days to their journey than walk through the "tainted" land of Samaria.

Jesus encountered this tension while He rested at a well in the village of Sychar in Samaria. When He asked a Samaritan woman for a drink, she asked incredulously, "How is it that You, being a Jew, ask me for a drink since I am a Samaritan woman?" (John 4:9). Certainly, the woman believed, no God-fearing Jew would have spoken to a Samaritan woman in broad daylight. That is, until Jesus came along.

In another astonishing scene, John describes a confrontation Jesus had with the Pharisees. They wrestled verbally with Him for claiming to be the Son of God. Jesus exclaimed:

> I speak the things which I have seen with My Father; there-
> fore you also do the things which you heard from *your*
> father. . . . But because I speak the truth, you do not
> believe Me. (John 8:38, 45, emphasis added)

At that, the Pharisees exclaimed:

> Do we not say rightly that You are a Samaritan and have a
> demon? (8:48)

The religious leaders' accusation dripped with prejudice. The Pharisees insulted Jesus with two of the worst terms they could think of—*Samaritan* and *demon*. And, yet, He was neither.

The Samaritan woman's words and the vicious verbal assaults of the Pharisees betray the fact that the first-century Jews had fallen into the grip of intense cultural prejudice. However, a more intense *political* prejudice existed between the Jewish people and the Romans.

Political Prejudice

In the first century, the people of Palestine struggled under Roman rule and suffered under their oppression. Not surprisingly, the Jewish people loathed the Romans for these things. To them, there was only One to whom they would pledge their allegiance as King—and it certainly wasn't Caesar. Their nation was a theocracy, ruled by Yahweh. Only His law was sacred to them. But the Jewish people still were forced to pay homage to the emperor of Rome.

And, as you can imagine, the Romans and the Jews despised each other.

In those days, the people were subjected to three taxes. First was a ground tax, which was one-tenth of everyone's grain and one-fifth of everyone's oil and wine, paid back in kind or in cash. Second was an income tax. Each person paid one percent of his or her income to Rome. Finally, a poll tax was taken. Every male aged fourteen to sixty-five and every female from age twelve to sixty-five paid a denarius (about a day's wage) to Caesar. The tribute coins that the people used to pay their taxes bore the mark of Caesar. The Pharisees tried to use the tax laws to trap Jesus:

> Then the Pharisees went and plotted together how they might trap Him in what He said. And they sent their disciples to Him, along with the Herodians, saying, "Teacher, we know that You are truthful and teach the way of God in truth, and defer to no one; for You are not partial to any. Tell us then, what do You think? Is it lawful to give a poll-tax to Caesar, or not?" But Jesus perceived their malice, and said, "Why are you testing Me, you hypocrites? Show Me the coin used for the poll-tax." And they brought Him a denarius. And He said to them, "Whose likeness and inscription is this?" They said to Him, "Caesar's." Then He said to them, "Then render to Caesar the things that are Caesar's; and to God the things that are God's." (Matthew 22:15–21)

What a brilliant answer! As Jesus held the Roman coin in His hand, He looked at the front and the back of it. The coin read, "Tiberius Caesar, son of the divine Augustus," on one side, and, "Pontiff Maximus, the High Priest," on the other. This second statement alone made the Pharisees' blood boil. In their minds, only the Jewish priest Caiaphas bore the title of High Priest—not Maximus, the pagan politician!

This scene helps us understand the intensity of the political prejudice prevalent in Jesus's day. But still another level of prejudice was present— religious prejudice in its most violent form.

Religious Prejudice

As the self-appointed guardians of religious purity (not *godly* purity), the Pharisees disdained those outside their group. Their words dripped with religious prejudice. They said concerning Jesus: "No one of the rulers or Pharisees has believed in Him, has he? But this crowd which does not know the Law is accursed" (John 7:48–49). They opposed any who threatened their carefully constructed religious system. Jesus, offering life instead of dead religion, posed the greatest threat.

Because of this, the Jewish religious leaders plotted to rid the land of Jesus and His followers. However, under Roman law, they lacked the authority to execute anyone. To have Jesus condemned to death, the Jewish leaders had to bring Jesus to Pilate, the Roman governor of Judea. They also had to "trump up" charges against Jesus. Why? According to Jewish law, to be guilty of blasphemy was punishable by death, but Roman law carried no such condemnation. So when Christ's accusers brought Him before the Roman authorities, they changed the accusation to treason. They contended that He was claiming to be king of the Jews, thus challenging Caesar. This charge became significant when Jesus appeared before Pilate, because anyone in Rome who attempted to set himself up to be king would be arrested and condemned to death.

PREJUDICE AT THE TRIALS AND CRUCIFIXION OF JESUS

No doubt, in Pilate's dealings with the Jewish leaders, he grew to loathe their self-righteous, petty religious ways. He also considered them inferior to the Romans. But Pilate was a "puppet" governor, operating under the threat of the Jews around him and the possibility of being removed from office because of so many complaints against him. He didn't always make the right choices, but he seemed to have a bit of respect for Jesus.

Strangely, Pilate was the only man who came anywhere close to giving Jesus an appropriate trial. He examined Him and found nothing wrong. Pilate realized that he was judging a man accused of crimes He hadn't committed. But Pilate was too weak and fearful to let Jesus go. He asked, "What evil has He done?" (Matthew 27:23). You can almost hear the desperation in his words. Finally, Pilate pleaded, "What shall I do with Jesus who is called Christ?" (27:22). The mob screamed back in response, "Crucify Him!" (27:22).

You wonder about the extent of prejudice? You just read it! Prejudice reduces the human spirit to the level of a killer beast.

How did Jesus endure the tough stuff of prejudice? He kept silent. He made no answer. He refused to defend Himself against false accusations. He even asked His Father to forgive those who treated Him with such cruel abuse and prejudice.

Scripture describes in graphic detail the painful prejudice that Jesus faced. How does the fact of His suffering make you feel?

_____

_____

_____

_____

Why do you think God allowed His Son to experience such great prejudice and face so many unfair accusations?

_____

_____

_____

_____

Three Observations About Prejudice

Prejudice is not limited to any particular region of the world or to a certain culture. It is a prevalent evil that plagues all people everywhere on every continent across the planet. Here are three observations that we can make regarding prejudice.

Prejudice is a learned trait. We weren't born prejudiced. Ever noticed that babies and young children will play with anyone who seems willing? They don't care if a person is white-skinned, black-skinned, blue-skinned, or anything in between! Only when we get older do we start to separate people into the categories of "more desirable" and "less desirable." We've *learned* to have prejudicial attitudes and feelings. We are taught prejudice by our peers, our parents, and our elders.

When a soldier finds himself engaged in a fierce battle, he quickly realizes that it doesn't matter whether the soldier next to him is male or female, black, Asian, white, Hispanic, or anything else. As long as that person can protect his or her fellow soldiers, no one engaged in the battle cares about skin color or cultural roots. The *perspective* changes because life and death hang in the balance. The soldiers' lives depend on trust and obedience, and they must band together to reach their common goal.

Prejudice blinds us in great darkness. In the book of Matthew, Jesus explained:

> The eye is the lamp of the body; so then if your eye is clear,
> your whole body will be full of light. But if your eye is bad,
> your whole body will be full of darkness. (Matthew 6:22–23)

Our eyes represent the windows of our body. They allow light to enter in, and that light forms images. Our brains then transform those images into thoughts, concepts, and ideas. This is not only true physically, but it's also true emotionally and spiritually.

If the eye sees a skin color that is different, clothing that seems unusual, or some cultural expression that it doesn't understand, a negative judgment may be formed. That judgment impacts the whole person who makes it—body, mind, and will. The mind of that person blindly bases its judgments on a reality that is only dimly perceived.

Prejudice binds us to the old. It is the ugliest side of traditionalism. You rarely find an extremely prejudiced person who is also positive, innovative, and creative. It's remarkable how creativity and innovation go along with a more progressive philosophy of life. Prejudice closes our minds to the possibility of the unusual. It holds our thoughts hostage in the vise grip of habit instead of freeing us to "think outside the box."

Jesus is here to offer His comforting presence and tender words of assurance when your faith falters under unfair discrimination and gross injustice.

TAKING TRUTH TO HEART

No doubt, your own experiences with prejudice have been painful. But the suffering that Christ experienced at the hands of hate-filled, prejudiced men boggles the mind. The perfect Son of God laid aside the independent and voluntary use of His divine attributes as He came to this earth to die, agreeing to pay the price for the sins of prejudiced people—not only theirs, but yours and mine. Amazing love—how can it be? All from a man who Himself never entertained one prejudicial thought.

Jesus knows the pain of prejudice's bite. He endured the curses and cruel remarks. He felt the shame of rejection. He experienced the shocking alienation of hatred. That had to hurt—even for Him.

Which people or groups do you tend to stereotype or harbor prejudices against? Why do you think this is the case?

_____

_____

_____

_____

_____

_____

Describe an instance when you mistakenly stereotyped someone or made a false assumption about him or her. What made you realize that your prejudices weren't true?

_____

_____

_____

_____

_____

_____

How do your prejudices prevent you from extending Christ's love to certain people?

_____

_____

_____

_____

_____

What lessons have you learned from your experiences with prejudice? How can you pass on these lessons to your loved ones so they can avoid being hurt or hurting others in the same way?

_____

_____

_____

_____

When you meet God in the tough stuff of prejudice, He will provide healing for you when others hurt and misjudge you. He also gently points out those blind spots in your own spiritual sight that keep you from seeing the truth. If you allow Him the freedom to do so, He will soften your spirit toward people of other colors, races, cultures, and belief systems.

eleven

GETTING THROUGH THE
TOUGH STUFF OF HYPOCRISY

Many people link Christianity with hypocrisy. One skeptic, Thomas R. Ybarra, wrote, "A Christian is a man who feels repentance on a Sunday for what he did on Saturday and is going to do on Monday."[1]

Sad, but often true. Today, it's not unusual for people to find a disconcerting connection between clergy and hypocrisy. An epidemic of abusive priests, fallen televangelists, and swindling ministers has all but obliterated what little trust people have left in church leaders.

But blatant phoniness among some religious leaders is nothing new. It also ran rampant in Jesus's day. He constantly confronted hypocrisy among the official Jewish leaders. In one of the messages that Jesus delivered, He denounced the religious establishment by repeating the same rebuke seven times: "Woe to you, scribes and Pharisees, hypocrites" (Matthew 23:13–15, 23, 25, 27, 29).

But Jesus's harsh condemnation didn't end there. He railed:

> Woe to you, blind guides, who say, "Whoever swears by the temple, that is nothing; but whoever swears by the gold of the temple is obligated." You fools and blind men! Which is more important, the gold or the temple that sanctified the gold? (Matthew 23:16–17)

That doesn't sound like "gentle Jesus, meek and mild," does it? Jesus displayed righteous anger and courage as He looked into the faces of these men and exposed their gross duplicity. Christ loathed the religious leaders' self-righteous piety because they said one thing but did another. They sounded righteous but were devoid of spiritual substance.

If we were completely honest with ourselves, you and I would have to own up to varying degrees of hypocrisy, too. We've all had to endure the tough stuff of fake faith—when we discover it either in ourselves or in someone we respect and trust. Only Jesus lived a perfectly righteous life, completely free of hypocrisy. That's why He's our model.

Name an example of hypocrisy that you have encountered. What were the circumstances?

_____

_____

_____

_____

_____

What bothered you so much about this situation? How did it change your feelings toward the person or people involved?

_____

_____

_____

_____

_____

GETTING TO THE ROOT

Jesus called the Pharisees and their religious colleagues "hypocrites." In Greek, the term is *hupokritēs*, which means, "one who answers, an actor, a hypocrite."[2] *Hupokritēs* referred to a type of Greek actor who would play multiple roles in a drama. He would disguise himself with a series of masks that he would interchange off stage, much to the audience's delight.

Webster defines *hypocrisy* as "a feigning to be what one is not or to believe what one does not; especially: the false assumption of an appearance of virtue or religion."[3]

Scripture condemns this type of pretending. God hates false piety, lack of authenticity, and duplicity of character. He decried hypocrisy in His people through the mouthpiece of the prophet Isaiah:

Because this people draw near with their words

And honor Me with their lip service,

But they remove their hearts far from Me,

And their reverence for Me consists of tradition learned

by rote,

> Therefore behold, I will once again deal marvelously with
> this people, wondrously marvelous;
> And the wisdom of their wise men will perish,
> And the discernment of their discerning men will be
> concealed. (Isaiah 29:13–14)

Not much has changed in the nearly twenty-seven hundred years since those words were proclaimed. We see an almost unending parade of hypocrisy in our churches today. And frankly, we can't blame unbelievers for tuning out many Christians. Nothing does more harm to the cause of Christ than hypocritical attitudes, words, and actions modeled by people who call themselves Christians. On the other hand, there is nothing like authenticity to disarm the person without Christ.

It's no wonder that Paul wrote to the believers in Rome with great fervor as he exhorted them to "let love be without hypocrisy" (Romans 12:9). He wanted their actions to match their words. He desired that the phony cloaks of religion be cast aside to make room for an authentic, vibrant, life-giving faith.

Peter fell into the trap of hypocrisy, too. Although he preached that all believers—both Jew and Gentile—were one in Christ, his conduct while ministering in Antioch didn't match his words. He wore two masks and was exposed by Paul's stinging rebuke (see Galatians 2:11–14).

TAKING TRUTH TO HEART

Hypocrisy occurs when we hide carnality behind a stack of religious words. That's phony. When wrestling with the tough stuff of hypocrisy, we need to listen to what Jesus said about it and allow Him to have His way in how we conduct ourselves each day.

In which areas of your life do you struggle to be authentic? What do you think makes it so difficult for you to be transparent and genuine in these particular areas?

_____

_____

_____

_____

Read Isaiah 29:13–14, Romans 12:9, and Galatians 2:11–14 again. According to these verses, what does God have to say to you about being more open and honest in the areas of your life in which you struggle with authenticity?

_____

_____

_____

_____

HYPOCRISY ILLUSTRATED

During His Sermon on the Mount, Jesus challenged His followers to live a life of simplicity and authenticity. He punctuated His call to genuine piety with a brief but bold exhortation:

> Beware of practicing your righteousness before men to be
> noticed by them; otherwise you have no reward with your
> Father who is in heaven. (Matthew 6:1)

In today's words, don't try to appear super-pious for the purpose of making yourself look good.

The Jews in Jesus's day believed in four fundamental ways of practicing righteousness: (1) giving, (2) praying, (3) fasting, and (4) embracing the religious traditions passed down to them by their elders. Jesus never disputed the importance of these disciplines. His concern was that these deeds of righteousness had become public platforms for hypocritical conduct, thanks to the example of the religious leaders. In place of this hypocritical sham, Jesus gave instructions on the right way to model each of these spiritual disciplines.

Giving

First, Jesus dealt with the matter of giving:

> So when you give to the poor, do not sound a trumpet
> before you, as the hypocrites do in the synagogues and in
> the streets, so that they may be honored by men. Truly I say
> to you, they have their reward in full. (Matthew 6:2)

Today, Jesus might tell you not to expect your church to name a building after you or to put your name on a commemorative plaque just because you wrote a large check. Don't be offended because your name doesn't appear in some public headline to honor your generosity. Don't give just to make yourself look good. Jesus offers a better way.

> But when you give to the poor, do not let your left hand know what your right hand is doing, so that your giving will be in secret; and your Father who sees what is done in secret will reward you. (Matthew 6:3–4)

Praying

Jesus also instructs us on the right way to pray:

> When you pray, you are not to be like the hypocrites; for they love to stand and pray in the synagogues and on the street corners so that they may be seen by men. Truly I say to you, they have their reward in full. (Matthew 6:5)

In Jesus's day, the practice of prayer had degenerated in five areas that needed correcting.

Prayer had become a formal exercise rather than a free expression. What existed were "official" prayers for all occasions. Prayers had become standardized, routine, and monotonous.

Prayer had grown ritualistic rather than authentic in its expression. The Pharisees instituted a rigid routine of prescribed places and set times for prayer. Most Jewish people prayed three times each day at the set hours of 9:00 a.m., 12:00 p.m., and 3:00 p.m. But very few people practiced spontaneous, spiritual prayer.

Prayers were long and wordy. The Pharisees believed that the more eloquent and flowery their prayers, the better. This was the accepted style when praying in public.

Prayers were filled with repetition and meaningless clichés. The religious leaders of Jesus's day cared more about sounding godly than they actually cared about being godly. They loved nothing more than to broadcast their prayers through the streets, repeating them over and over for emphasis.

Praying became a cause for pride rather than an opportunity to express humble reliance on God. The religious leaders prayed in order to receive the admiration and praise of men rather than to give their admiration and praise to God for all He had done for them.

Thankfully, Jesus did not leave us to flounder in our own struggle to overcome hypocritical prayer. He taught us:

> But you, when you pray, go into your inner room, close your door and pray to your Father who is in secret, and your Father who sees what is done in secret will reward you.
>
> And when you are praying, do not use meaningless repetition as the Gentiles do, for they suppose that they will be heard for their many words. (Matthew 6:6–7)

Isn't it good when we approach the Lord and talk to Him naturally? If some of our children spoke to their dads like we talk to God, we'd laugh out loud. "O great, delightful, good, and loving earthly father. What is it that thou dost wish me to do?" If you want to get back to the basics of authentic prayer, think back to your first feeble prayers as a new believer. These prayers were wonderfully spontaneous, real, personal, and honest—just straight, pure talk that thrilled the heart of God.

Fasting

Next, Jesus dealt with fasting, another discipline in which hypocrisy flourished:

> Whenever you fast, do not put on a gloomy face as the hypocrites do, for they neglect their appearance so that they will be noticed by men when they are fasting. Truly I say to you, they have their reward in full. (Matthew 6:16)

Picture the following scenario in your mind:

> The Jewish days of fasting were Monday and Thursday. These were market days, and . . . the result was that those who were ostentatiously fasting would on those days have a bigger audience to see and admire their piety. There were many who took deliberate steps to see that others could not miss the fact that they were fasting. They walked through the streets with hair deliberately unkempt and dishevelled, with clothes deliberately soiled and disarrayed. They even went the length of deliberately whitening their faces to accentuate their paleness. This was no act of humility; it was a deliberate act of spiritual pride and ostentation.[4]

Showing off spiritually is blatant hypocrisy, which is precisely why Jesus warned against it. How, then, are we to fast before the Lord? Let's hear the answer from Eugene Peterson's paraphrase of Matthew 6:16–18.

> When you practice some appetite-denying discipline to better concentrate on God, don't make a production out of it. It might turn you into a small-time celebrity but it won't make you a saint. If you "go into training" inwardly, act normal outwardly. Shampoo and comb your hair, brush your teeth, wash your face. God doesn't require attention-getting devices. He won't overlook what you are doing; he'll reward you well. (MSG)

Embracing Tradition

Jesus confronted one final area of hypocrisy in the conduct of the Pharisees and other religious leaders—embracing and clinging to meaningless traditions.

> Then some Pharisees and scribes came to Jesus from Jeru-salem and said, "Why do Your disciples break the tradition of the elders? For they do not wash their hands when they eat bread." (Matthew 15:1–2)

The Pharisees and scribes were first-century, card-carrying legalists. They upheld a tradition of their own that required elaborate hand washing before meals and between each of the courses. Water was poured on each hand in a particular way and allowed to drip from the hands, making the hands "clean" and the water "unclean."

It would have been easier just to skip the meal than to do all this meticulous hand washing! Jesus immediately spotted the hypocrisy in the hearts of these men and wasted no words in His firm rebuke:

> Why do you yourselves transgress the commandment of God for the sake of your tradition? For God said, "Honor your father and mother," and, "He who speaks evil of his father or mother is to be put to death." But you say, "Whoever says to his father or mother, 'Whatever I have that would help you has been given to God,' he is not to honor his father or his mother." And by this you invalidate the word of God for the sake of your tradition. You hypocrites, rightly did Isaiah prophesy of you:
>
> "This people honors Me with their lips,
> But their heart is far from Me.
> But in vain do they worship Me,
> Teaching as doctrines the precepts of men."
> (Matthew 15:3–9)

The treacherous part about embracing tradition over Scripture is that it *invalidates* the Word of God. When we give people lists to live by, they'll be tempted to follow the lists more rigidly than they follow what the Bible commands.

In which ways do Christians today still focus on the externals of "practicing righteousness"?

_____

_____

_____

_____

Take a minute to think about why you participate in spiritual practices such as prayer, fasting, service, or Scripture reading. Do you engage in these disciplines to gain recognition for yourself or to seek the heart of the Father?

_____

_____

_____

_____

How do the motivations you uncovered above line up with Jesus's teaching on the subject? (See Matthew 6:1–7, 16–18, and 15:1–9.)

_____

_____

_____

_____

In the space below, write out a short prayer confessing your hypocrisy to God. Ask the Lord to renew your spirit and help you live out an authentic faith that pleases Him.

_____

_____

_____

_____

THREE PRINCIPLES FOR OVERCOMING HYPOCRISY

Three principles will help us overcome hypocritical tendencies in our own lives and in the conduct of others.

Exposing hypocrisy is helpful; reveal it! Address it with your children, especially those who are homeschooled or enrolled in Christian schools. They're getting maximum doses of teaching on externals, but they also need to hear lessons on grace, authenticity, honesty, and forgiveness. Without a necessary balance, your children can get the wrong message and develop convictions that don't align with Scripture.

Practicing hypocrisy is natural; resist it! Hypocritical conduct comes as naturally to Christians as breathing. It appeals to our old nature. We get hooked on it because our hypocritical behavior often brings us praise, and we end up looking quite godly and impressive. But in reality, hypocrisy represents the ugly underbelly of our faith, and therefore we must resist it.

Breaking with hypocrisy is painful; stay at it! It's much easier to mentor a brand-new Christian than one who's steeped in years of religion and churchy traditionalism. Stamping out hypocrisy can be a long, difficult process. But it's worth it!

List several practical ways that you can put these three principles into practice and help eliminate hypocrisy from your life.

_____

_____

_____

_____

Winning any personal battle starts with an admission of the problem. Only then can the Holy Spirit begin a work of deliverance that will put us on a path of genuine freedom from hypocrisy. Overcoming the destructive power of false religiosity begins when we are completely unguarded and honest with ourselves and with God. There's no hedging allowed, no blaming our sins on our past, and no pinning the responsibility for our problems on anyone else. Doing this will be tough, but take heart! We have the resources of heaven on our side.

twelve

GETTING THROUGH THE
TOUGH STUFF OF INADEQUACY

Feelings of inadequacy are inextricably bound to our identity as frail, fallible humans. Like parasites, these feelings feed on our shortcomings and failures. They thrive on our infirmities, constantly humbling us, continually pushing us down when we want so much to rise above.

Have you ever felt so inadequate that you were convinced you couldn't go on? Usually, we feel most inadequate when we've been used or exploited by somebody else or when we feel that we simply don't measure up to someone else's standards. At times, feelings of inadequacy can run so deep we wish we could just disappear. Life's challenges can seem too great when we feel inadequate to

- meet the needs of our families;

- fulfill the demands of our jobs;

- face the emotional demands of a romance or friendship;

- care for a child with special needs;

- perform our ministries;

- keep going physically in spite of chronic pain;

- care for our husband and several young children;

- be a superhero to our wife and kids;

- care for our aging parents.

Let's face it: *To be human is to feel inadequate at times.* So let's figure out how to deal with inadequacy's negative messages and how to overcome them in the power of the Holy Spirit.

GETTING TO THE ROOT

What does it mean to be "inadequate"? First, let's look at what it means to be adequate. The Greek word for adequate, *hikanos,* means "to reach or attain, or to be sufficient, fit, or able."[1] To be adequate means that we have sufficient ability and resources to meet a certain requirement. It means we're fit and able to accomplish a given task. To be inadequate, then, means just the opposite—that we're incapable and without the necessary abilities or skills to complete a task.

Most of us disguise our inadequacies because we don't like to admit to ourselves, let alone to our peers, that we are weak and incapable. Instead, we pretend that we've got it all together. We act as if we are capable of handling the most challenging situations in life when, in fact, we aren't. Basically, we're powerless to overcome most of what we will face in this world. And there's a simple reason: *God made us this way.*

Why Inadequacy Exists

Few people in the Bible struggled with inadequacy to such depths as the apostle Paul. That may surprise you, but it's absolutely true. In his own words, he admitted that he rarely felt up to the task. As the great apostle contemplated the eternal consequences of his ministry, he struggled with intense feelings of inadequacy.

> For we are a fragrance of Christ to God among those who are being saved and among those who are perishing; to the one an aroma from death to death, to the other an aroma from life to life. And who is adequate for these things? (2 Corinthians 2:15–16)

Truth be told, people are not adequate in themselves—not you, not me, not even Paul. Nevertheless, he enjoyed remarkable ministry success. So how did this happen? Where did he get his power? He answered this question when he wrote,

> Not that we are adequate in ourselves to consider any-
> thing as coming from ourselves, but *our adequacy is from*
> *God.* (2 Corinthians 3:5, emphasis added)

Don't miss those last five words! *Our adequacy is from God.* Without God and the power He pours into us, we're incapable of doing anything praiseworthy. All of us are weak at times—emotionally, spiritually, intellectually, and physically. We don't possess the capacity to glorify God in and of ourselves. In our own strength, we can't do His work. If we are going to be His hands and feet, His voice and His presence, His salt and light in the world, it will happen only as He works through us. That's why God allows us to experience feelings of inadequacy. Inadequacy forces us to rely on Him fully for power and strength.

In which areas of your life do you currently feel the most inadequate?

_____

_____

_____

_____

_____

Why do you think this is the case?

_____

_____

_____

_____

_____

TAKING TRUTH TO HEART

Maybe you can identify with the feelings of one pastor's wife, who wrote these words a number of years ago:

> My husband and I have occasionally felt on the edge of an ill-defined despair. Those were times when we felt a variety of things: a desire either to quit or run, a feeling of anger, the temptation to fight back at someone, the sense of being used or exploited, the weakness of inadequacy, and the reality of loneliness. Such attitudes can easily conspire to reduce the strongest and the most gifted to a state of nothingness.[2]

None of us can escape the limitations of our humanity. Maybe that's why the Bible exhorts Christians to anticipate heaven, to look forward to that day when we'll be glorified—fully complete in Christ and finally fulfilled in our heavenly home. But the fact remains that while we remain earthbound, we'll continually struggle with what it means to be human—to feel inadequate to face life's demands and challenges.

INADEQUATE FOR THE TASK GOD GIVES

Like Paul, the disciples realized how ill equipped they were to begin a worldwide ministry. Their sense of inadequacy only intensified as they shouldered the guilt and shame of deserting Jesus. Still, after the Resurrection, Jesus commissioned them to make disciples of all nations. How could a rough-edged, unsophisticated band of followers become instruments of power to fulfill a humanly impossible mission? A closer look at Scripture will help us answer that question.

A Study in Contrasts

Following the Resurrection, the disciples met Jesus in Galilee. Matthew, one of the faithful eleven, recalled what transpired when he wrote:

> But the eleven disciples proceeded to Galilee, to the mountain which Jesus had designated. When they saw Him, they worshiped Him; but some were doubtful. (Matthew 28:16–17)

Think of the contrasts between Jesus and His disciples. On one hand, you find eleven trembling, confused, and doubting disciples. On the other hand stands the all-powerful, completely adequate risen Lord. The men were human—limited, weak, feeble, frail, and prone to failure. Jesus was God's promised Messiah—fully human, fully divine, omniscient, omnipresent, and all-sufficient.

The group of disciples included Peter, who had denied Jesus; Matthew, a former tax collector; and a couple of hot-tempered fishermen from Galilee. The disciples had feared a raging storm on the Sea of Galilee, but Jesus had commanded the wind and the waves to be still. The disciples had run for their lives out of the Garden of Gethsemane, but Jesus had faced His death with undaunted resolve. The eleven men weren't subpar in intelligence, and they didn't lack zeal, love, or devotion. They were just human, and therefore, inadequate for the task. But that was about to change.

A Command and a Promise

Before we look down on the disciples for their insufficiency or inadequacy, let's admit that if we had been in their place, we might have been doubtful, too. Their hopes had been dashed when they heard their Master breathe His last on the cross. The whole mystery of His miraculous, bodily resurrection had yet to work itself out in their confused minds. Uncertainties and unanswered questions lingered. However, Christ's plan for them would provide not only clear answers to their questions but also the needed solution to their shortcomings.

> And Jesus came up and spoke to them, saying, "All authority has been given to Me in heaven and on earth. Go therefore and make disciples of all the nations, baptizing them in the name of the Father and the Son and the Holy Spirit, teaching them to observe all that I commanded you; and lo, I am with you always, even to the end of the age." (Matthew 28:18–20)

Jesus had given the disciples a command to "make disciples of all the nations." But to do that, they had to forsake everything. They must have buckled under the weight of such a mammoth assignment. They weren't equipped to perform miracles as Christ was. They couldn't read the hearts and thoughts of men as He could. How could they possibly accomplish all that He expected of them? And He was going away soon! Sure, He had promised never to leave them and to grant them His own heavenly authority. But would that be enough? They needed more than a command and a promise. They needed to receive an infusion of power—*His* power! And no one knew that better than Jesus.

His Power Made Perfect in Weakness

Luke, the writer of the book of Acts, picks up where the Gospels leave off—after the Resurrection but before Christ's ascension to heaven. Read Luke's words slowly and thoughtfully, as though you're encountering them for the first time. As you do, remember that the disciples had just received their commission and were likely fighting off debilitating feelings of personal and collective inadequacy.

> Gathering them together, He commanded them not to leave Jerusalem, but to wait for what the Father had promised, "Which," He said, "you heard of from Me; for John baptized with water, but you will be baptized with the Holy Spirit not many days from now. . . . But you will receive power when the Holy Spirit has come upon you; and you shall be My witnesses both in Jerusalem, and in all Judea and Samaria, and even to the remotest part of the earth." (Acts 1:4–5, 8)

Jesus was asking the impossible of this tiny band of reluctant evangelists. But that was precisely the point. They needed His power to accomplish His command. They needed to be *transformed*. And so do we!

Christ has given us His power through the abiding presence of the Holy Spirit. The Holy Spirit indwells us when we turn to God through faith in His Son. We don't have to dance, jump, shout, or plead in order to receive divine power. If you have made the decision to become a true follower of Christ, you already have His power within you. The Holy Spirit literally resides within your being. The more you yield your life to Him, the more His power flows through you.

Back in the first century, the disciples were to wait in Jerusalem for the Spirit's power to descend upon them. It would be the very same power they saw at work in Jesus's miraculous life. It would be a power strong enough to transform these men—men once dominated by inadequacy and fear—into bold, courageous, and capable witnesses for Christ. Talk about *transformed!*

Acts 2 records the amazing event when the Spirit came as promised, appearing as tongues of fire. The disciples experienced complete spiritual transformation. Were they still men—mere humans? Yes. But deep within their beings, they received the empowering Holy Spirit that worked through them to turn the world upside down.

TWO PRINCIPLES FOR OVERCOMING INADEQUACY

These two simple principles can help you apply Christ's power to your inadequacy.

First, admit your inadequacies. This is the initial step toward accepting God's power. Few people ever overcome the struggle of a deep, debilitating sense of inadequacy without first acknowledging their need for God's help. That's true of drug addicts, sex addicts, alcoholics, gamblers, hotheads, procrastinators, perfectionists, fretters, worriers, the abusive, the impatient, the fearful, the depressed, and the disobedient. The category of the weakness doesn't matter. As a matter of fact, the more impossible it seems to overcome your weakness, the better. That's when you and I are most likely to acknowledge our desperate need for God's power.

If you're too proud to admit your need and ask God for His help, your feelings of inadequacy will continue to control you. It's that simple. The apostle Paul knew the power that lay in bringing his weakness to the Lord and, therefore, he humbly admitted his need for God's power.

Read 1 Corinthians 2:1–4. How did Paul's weaknesses manifest themselves?

_____

_____

_____

_____

What gave Paul the power to minister effectively despite his weaknesses?

_____

_____

_____

_____

Now, read 2 Corinthians 4:7. In what type of vessel does our treasure reside? How would you translate this metaphor into modern terms?

_____

_____

_____

_____

What is the purpose of our inadequacies, according to this verse?

_____

_____

_____

_____

How can you apply these spiritual truths to your own insecurities and inadequacies?

_____

_____

_____

_____

Now, read Paul's personal story, which explains how he acknowledged his inadequacies and found them to be God's way of using him even more effectively:

> I was given the gift of a handicap to keep me in constant touch with my limitations. Satan's angel did his best to get me down; what he in fact did was push me to my knees. No danger then of walking around high and mighty! At first I didn't think of it as a gift, and begged God to remove it. Three times I did that, and then he told me,

My grace is enough; it's all you need.

My strength comes into its own in your

weakness.

Once I heard that, I was glad to let it happen. I quit focusing
on the handicap and began appreciating the gift. It was a case
of Christ's strength moving in on my weakness. Now I take
limitations in stride, and with good cheer, these limitations
that cut me down to size—abuse, accidents, opposition, bad
breaks. I just let Christ take over! And so the weaker I get,
the stronger I become. (2 Corinthians 12:7–10, MSG)

What was Paul's initial reaction to his infirmity and inadequacy?

_____

_____

_____

_____

*How did his perspective change over time? How was he able to accept his weakness and
even celebrate and thank God for it?*

_____

_____

_____

_____

What might God be teaching you through your own inadequacies?

_____

_____

_____

_____
_____

_____

Paul remains one of the most self-effacing and self-denying servants the church has ever known. Like few before him and few since, he understood the power of the Holy Spirit to make him adequate to complete God's assignment for him. He recognized that no matter how long you have walked with the Savior, no matter how big your church is, and no matter how much you give to the ministry, it is *God* that makes you adequate. "But our adequacy is from God" (2 Corinthians 3:5). Never forget that!

Second, to overcome inadequacey, claim Christ's power. Christ's power is the ultimate secret to living above the level of mediocrity, including spiritual mediocrity. God does His best work in our weakness. That's His plan. We don't have to pretend to be super-strong, self-assertive, self-reliant people in order for Him to use us. In fact, He prefers us to be humble, teachable, and moldable, like clay in the hands of a skillful potter. God uses weak, trembling, inadequate, ill-equipped people—people just like you and me. There's hope for us after all!

If you've been wallowing in your inadequacies, it's time for you to kneel before God and let go of them. He's waiting to demonstrate His great power in you. Don't waste another minute trying get through the tough stuff of inadequacy on your own. Run to Him and receive the power that He grants through the Holy Spirit. Remember the words of the apostle Paul. Stop focusing on your inability, and start appreciating what God can do through you with His power.

thirteen

GETTING THROUGH THE
TOUGH STUFF OF DISQUALIFICATION

You've probably heard the statistics. One in every two churchgoers is actively involved with Internet pornography. That's *50 percent of people who claim to be Christians.* Nine out of ten children between the ages of eight and sixteen have been exposed to Internet pornography accidentally while doing their homework online. And an incredible 37 percent of *pastors* say that Internet porn is a current struggle in their own lives!

When a minister fails and falls, the impact is scandalous. Certainly his sinful choices deeply affect his family, his congregation, and his entire community. But *any* Christian's fall diminishes the cause of Christ. Remember what happened in elementary school when someone was caught cheating at a game? He or she was disqualified from playing and had to sit on the sidelines.

The same thing happens when we fall into immorality or other sin. It undercuts our credibility to speak the gospel. It disqualifies us from being respected, it disqualifies us from impacting others, and it disqualifies us from serving as role models.

The threat of disqualification among members of the body of Christ is serious business. If you know Christ as Savior and Lord, you can never lose your guarantee of heaven or the promise of His forgiveness and grace. Yours is an eternal salvation once you've trusted in Christ by faith. But you can, on the other hand, lose the magnificent privilege of serving Him in public places of ministry. Certain sinful choices could cause you to lose your integrity in the eyes of those around you and could severely damage your testimony. We need to live with a healthy fear of being disqualified. All Christians are susceptible to enemy attack, and the battle is only getting fiercer.

Two Biblical Word Pictures of How We're to Live

As Salt and Light

So, what is our life supposed to be like if we're running to win the eternal prize? Jesus said that we're to be like salt and light to the world (Matthew 5:13–16). By living a life of abundant faith, we should create a thirst for God in others. That's what Christ meant by being *salt*. Salt has a preserving quality, and without it, food loses its flavor.

Jesus also underscored the fact that believers must be *light* (5:14). When we shine brightly, we dispel spiritual darkness. Tragically, the world is full of lights that once burned brightly but have since flickered out. Each of us can make a difference by living rightly and offering light in "the midst of a crooked and perverse generation" (Philippians 2:15). Unless we live differently from nonbelievers, we run the risk of being disqualified.

How can you sprinkle your salt and shine your light in a flavorless and dark world?

_____

_____

_____

_____

As a Well-Trained Athlete

As Christians, we're called to train and discipline ourselves to do what's right. The apostle Paul himself lived with a healthy fear of being disqualified, of doing something that would counteract or nullify the work of the gospel. He not only erected safeguards against the enemy, he also disciplined himself for battle. He likened this training program to an athlete's.

We all know that successful athletes aren't just born that way. They cultivate their abilities and skills through disciplined practice. Paul provided a vivid word picture of a person who disciplines his body and mind in order to lead an effective Christian life:

> Do you not know that those who run in a race all run, but only one receives the prize? Run in such a way that you may win. Everyone who competes in the games exercises self-control in all things. They then do it to receive a perishable wreath, but we an imperishable. Therefore I run in such a way, as not without aim; I box in such a way, as not beating the air; but I discipline my body and make it my slave, so that, after I have preached to others, *I myself will not be disqualified.* (1 Corinthians 9:24–27, emphasis added)

GETTING TO THE ROOT

The Greek word translated "disqualified," *adokimos*, means "not standing the test; rejected."[1] In the ancient Greek culture, few things brought more shame on a community than having its star athlete disqualified from competition. One author writes, "An examination of the combatants took place after the contest. And if it could be proved that they had contended unlawfully or unfairly, they were deprived of the prize and driven with disgrace from the games."[2] No more shameful act could happen to a community than to have their star athlete *adokimos*.

Paul anticipated winning the prize, but he also understood the sacrifice that was required to receive it: a life well-lived, free from behaviors and attitudes that would disqualify him.

Are you currently an athlete, or did you play sports in your younger years? If so, which sports? Perhaps you played an instrument or cultivated some other skill. What specific types of training and discipline were required to excel at your sport or activity?

_____

_____

_____

_____

_____

_____

_____

_____

How can you apply the same principles of practice and discipline to your spiritual life? List several specific ways.

_____

_____

_____

_____

_____

_____

AN OLD TESTAMENT WARNING

Perhaps Paul had a flash of insight when he wrote to warn the Corinthian believers about disqualification. He knew that those who love God and commit their lives to the pursuit of spiritual things are at an increased risk of failure due to overexposure to God's blessings. An illustration from the Old Testament came to him as a fitting picture of the perils of overexposure:

> For I do not want you to be unaware, brethren, that our fathers were all under the cloud and all passed through the sea; and all were baptized into Moses in the cloud and in the sea; and all ate the same spiritual food; and all drank the same spiritual drink, for they were drinking from a spiritual rock which followed them; and the rock was Christ. (1 Corinthians 10:1–4)

The Israelites were living the high life under God's generous provisions and sheltering cloud. God had led them on the Exodus and continued to guide them on their journey to the Promised Land. Surely, these Israelites carried out their responsibility to live holy lives. Right? Unfortunately, no. Paul wrote:

> Nevertheless, with most of them God was not well-pleased;
>
> for they were laid low in the wilderness. (1 Corinthians 10:5)

As a result of God's displeasure, most of the Israelites never reached the Promised Land. Instead, they died and were buried in the wilderness.

If you had lived as a Hebrew in that generation when Moses stood against Pharaoh, you would have realized that you were one of God's chosen people. You would have been "under the cloud" (10:1), enjoying *supernatural guidance.* You would have been among those who "passed through the sea" (10:1), thereby experiencing *supernatural deliverance.* You would have gloried in the blessings of being a part of Moses's flock—benefiting from his remarkable giftedness and *supernatural leadership.* You would have had ample food and water and counted yourself part of a people destined for God's rich blessings.

But in spite of all of this, the Israelites started to complain. Eventually, they became bitter, taking God's goodness for granted. So they were "laid low" in the wilderness (10:5). God *disqualified* them by preventing that entire generation (except Joshua and Caleb) from ever setting foot in the Promised Land.

In a somber tone, Paul drove home his major concern, reminding us:

> Now these things happened to them as an example, and
>
> they were written for our instruction, upon whom the
>
> ends of the ages have come. (1 Corinthians 10:11)

GETTING TO THE ROOT

The Greek word translated "example" in verse 11 is *tupikos*, which comes from the root word *tupos*, meaning a "mark . . . an impression, or a stamp (made by a die)."[3] The negative example of the Israelites should stamp its indelible impression on our minds, continually reminding us of the cost of rebelling against God.

What spiritual lessons can you glean from the negative example of the Israelites?

_____

_____

_____

_____

_____

_____

THE DOWNWARD SPIRAL OF DISQUALIFICATION

How did God's chosen people come to be laid low in the wilderness? How do Christians today, blessed with so much—including the Holy Spirit—get caught in the snare of disqualification? It happens in much the same way an Eskimo hunts and kills a wolf. (Be prepared to shudder! The following account from Paul Harvey is grisly, yet it provides important insight into the destructive nature of sin.)

First, the Eskimo coats his knife blade with animal blood and allows it to freeze. Then he adds another layer of blood, and another, until the blade is completely concealed by frozen blood. Next, the hunter pushes the handle of his knife in the snow, blade up. When a wolf follows its nose to the source of the scent, it begins to lick the knife blade, tasting the frozen blood. The licking accelerates as the wolf laps against the blade until the keen edge is bare. So great becomes its craving for blood that the wolf does not notice the sting of the sharp blade on its own tongue, nor does the animal recognize that its thirst is being satisfied by its own warm blood. The carnivorous wolf just craves more—until the dawn finds it dead in the blood-soaked snow.[4]

Disqualification follows the same pattern. Silent temptations bombard our minds. Left unchecked, these temptations grow until we choose to act on them. Then, it's too late. We've been disqualified.

Paul traced the downward spiral of sin in the lives of the Israelites, issuing stern warnings:

Now these things happened as examples for us, so that we would not crave evil things as they also craved. Do not be idolaters, as some of them were; as it is written, "The people sat down to eat and drink, and stood up to play." Nor let us act immorally, as some of them did, and twenty-three thousand fell in one day. Nor let us try the Lord, as some of them did, and were destroyed by the serpents.

Nor grumble, as some of them did, and were destroyed by
the destroyer. (1 Corinthians 10:6–10)

Let's take a look at each of these elements of sin so we can learn how to prevent disqualification in our own lives.

Avoid craving evil things (10:6). Drifting starts with a craving for evil things. We are consumed by our own sinful desires until suddenly we find ourselves out of control and longing for more. Our craving may be for a sinful involvement with another person. It could be for Internet pornography or any type of sin—all of them specially designed to disqualify us from being an effective witness for Christ.

Avoid becoming idolaters (10:7). Idolatry occurs when we put something else in the place of God. Usually, we don't plan to be idolators; rather, we grow into it. Idolatry develops from a secret dethroning of Christ in our lives. It happens when we habitually preoccupy ourselves with our sin or something or someone beside Him. Like erosion, idolatry makes no noise and attracts little attention, but over time it leads to utter destruction.

Avoid acting immorally (10:8). The word translated "immorality" comes from the Greek root *pornos*, which means "fornication." Sexual immorality was rampant in the time of the Exodus, just as it was in first-century Corinth and is today. It's accepted and paraded before us, so we have to arm ourselves against it to prevent it from consuming our thoughts.

Avoid "trying the Lord" (10:9). Next, we come to the point where we mentally shake our fists at God. This is the sin of presumption—taking willful advantage of God's grace, presuming on His longsuffering, and dancing near the edge of disaster.

Avoid grumbling against God (10:10). Unbelievably, God's people, who had enjoyed His glorious deliverance and excellent provisions, got to the point where they did nothing but complain in the desert. Their sin blinded them to God's abundant grace, and they became bitter because some of their fleshly desires were unfulfilled.

Like stepping stones leading to destruction, these five elements can lead us down the painful path of disqualification.

RESPONDING TO SPIRITUAL DANGER GOD'S WAY

Paul realized that his readers would respond in one of two ways. Some would say, "This would never happen to *me!*" He warned them, "Let him who thinks he stands take heed that he does not fall" (1 Corinthians 10:12). In other words, no one is immune to disqualification. Anyone can fall. Therefore, we should each heed every warning the Scripture provides. We're *all* in peril of being disqualified.

On the other hand, some will say, "I'm in so deep I can never get out. The mess I've made of my life is too great for me even to hope for recovery. It's too late for me." To them, Paul wrote,

> No temptation has overtaken you but such as is common to man; and God is faithful, who will not allow you to be tempted beyond what you are able, but with the temptation will provide the way of escape also, so that you will be able to endure it. (1 Corinthians 10:13)

Did you catch that? God is faithful, and *He always provides us a way of escape.* We're never forced to sin. We're never forced into being disqualified. We always have a choice. When we trust God and cling to Him in faith, He'll give us the strength to resist temptation. What a gracious and compassionate God we have!

What hope for facing trials can you gain from Paul's words in 1 Corinthians 10:13?

_____

_____

_____

_____

_____

TAKING TRUTH TO HEART

Take a moment to ask yourself the following questions:

1. *Have you continued to maintain your walk with God, or have you lost your first love?*

2. *If your love has faded, can you locate the place where spiritual erosion began to occur? Are you willing to address it and come to terms with it?*

3. *Do you realize the danger of continuing on, unwilling to change? Can you see yourself in the downward spiral talked about earlier?*

4. *Especially if you are engaged in Christian service, are you aware of those who are watching you and counting on you to stand true? Are you fully aware of the devastating impact of failing them?*

We've all fallen into temptation at some point. However, it's never too late to start doing the right thing! Repent and confess to God your failure to obey and your inability to change on your own. Ask for His strength to overcome your sin. Stop rationalizing what you're doing. Don't go another day without crying out to God like the psalmist David:

> Create in me a clean heart, O God,
> And renew a steadfast spirit within me. . . .
> Restore to me the joy of Your salvation
> And sustain me with a willing spirit. (Psalm 51:10, 12)

In which areas of your life do you feel you're most susceptible to disqualification? List them here. Then, take time to pray and ask God to create in you a clean heart with regard to these areas.

_____

_____

_____

_____

_____

_____

_____

_____

_____

_____

There's no such thing as a sudden "spiritual blowout" in the Christian life. Every failure begins with a series of small, imperceptible leaks in the lining of our character. Though the final act of falling may be sudden and disastrous, it brings with it a lingering past of poor choices and reminders that we entertained temptation before we took the fall. But thankfully, we can choose the path that leads us back to God's tender mercies. God awaits the return of any prodigal son or daughter with open arms. He'll help you get back into the race and run it like you've never run before.

fourteen

GETTING THROUGH THE TOUGH STUFF OF DEATH

Joseph Bayly knew about death. He experienced its sting too many times. His newborn son died after surgery, his five-year-old son died from leukemia, and his eighteen-year-old son was killed in a sledding accident complicated by mild hemophilia. Each encounter taught Bayly a different lesson about the painful reality of death. In his book *The Last Thing We Talk About,* he wrote:

> The hearse began its grievous journey many thousand years ago, as a litter made of saplings.
>
> Litter, sled, wagon, Cadillac: the conveyance has changed, but the corpse it carries is the same.
>
> Birth and death enclose man in a sort of parenthesis of the present. And the brackets at the beginning and end of life are still impenetrable.

This frustrates us, especially in a time of scientific break-through and exploding knowledge, that we should be able to break out of earth's environment and yet be stopped cold by death's unyielding mystery. Electroencephalogram may replace a mirror held before the mouth, autopsies may become more sophisticated, cosmetic embalming may take the place of pennies on the eyelids and canvas shrouds, but death continues to confront us with its blank wall. Everything changes; death is changeless. . . .

Dairy farmer and sales executive live in death's shadow, with Nobel Prize winner and prostitute, mother, infant, teen, old man. The hearse stands waiting for the surgeon who transplants a heart as well as the hopeful recipient, for the funeral director as well as the corpse he manipulates.

Death spares none.[1]

Sobering words, written by one who had become all too familiar with death. Few people willingly face their own mortality, let alone talk openly about it. In fact, people have many peculiar ways of coping with the subject of death. Let's look at some of the more familiar ways that people deal with this difficult reality.

FOUR COMMON REACTIONS TO DEATH

Many people try to mask the solemnity of death with *humor*. A bumper sticker that appeared several years ago says it all: "Don't take life so seriously! You won't get out of it alive anyway." Too often, people handle death by trying to keep the subject humorous. Woody Allen once quipped, "It's not that I'm afraid to die. I just don't want to be there when it happens."[2] Somehow, making a joke about death helps to keep it at a safe distance. Then we never have to face its stark, painful reality.

Another familiar reaction to death is *denial.* Instead of talking about death, people try to deny it and remove the subject from all conversation. It's easier for us not to talk about death's reality than to wrestle with its meaning. That's why we purchase *life* insurance instead of *death* insurance. Let's face it—who wants to buy *death* coverage? Life is a much easier sell!

Others choose to *romanticize* death by emphasizing its supposed beauty with elaborate flower arrangements and graceful hymns. There's certainly nothing wrong with having a proper ceremony and memorial tribute to honor one who has died. But we can't gloss over the pain of those final good-byes with beautiful bouquets and moving poetry.

Perhaps the most common reaction to death is *fear.* People fear death like few other realities. If you don't think people are afraid to die, observe how your fellow passengers on an airplane react when severe air turbulence causes the plane to dip and jerk violently during a flight. Young and old alike gasp and cling to their armrests in fear.

Describe a time in your life when you had to face the tough stuff of death. How did this experience affect you emotionally, physically, and spiritually?

_____

_____

_____

_____

How do you deal with the idea of your own death or the death of a loved one? Do you tend to respond with humor, denial, romanticism, or fear? Why do you think you react this way?

_____

_____

_____

_____

_____

Sooner or later, we'll all face death. When you or a loved one is dying, death will not be funny or deniable or romantic. But it need not be fearful, either. Let's turn to John 11 and see how Jesus helped two sisters, Mary and Martha, cope with their brother's death.

A POIGNANT STORY OF GRIEF AND DEATH

Sickness Turns to Death

No laughter rang through the house of Mary, Martha, and Lazarus in Bethany that day. An ominous cloud of uncertainty hung heavy over the home where Lazarus lay dying.

> Now a certain man was sick, Lazarus of Bethany, the village
> of Mary and her sister Martha. (John 11:1)

Without warning, Lazarus had fallen desperately ill. Doctors came and went, shaking their heads in bewilderment. Lazarus's condition grew more and more grim. Lazarus, along with his sisters, Martha and Mary, enjoyed a close friendship with Jesus, so the sisters called on Jesus in their despair:

> The sisters sent word to Him, saying, "Lord, behold, he whom You love is sick." (John 11:3)

Mary and Martha knew that if anyone could help, it was the Master. Surely He would drop everything and rush to Bethany to help His dear friend, wouldn't He? But He didn't. In fact, Jesus stayed right where He was. And Lazarus's condition deteriorated even further.

Jesus deliberately chose not to go to Bethany right away. He didn't even go the next day—or the next. And, just as Mary and Martha had feared, Lazarus died.

Besides their intense grief at their brother's death, Mary and Martha harbored feelings of bitterness and anger toward Jesus. They had expected Him to arrive in time to heal their brother before the disease took its deadly toll. But the Savior didn't show up.

Playing the Blame Game

News of Lazarus's death finally reached Jesus. Back in Bethany, Mary and Martha's friends had come from all over the region to mourn with the bereaved women (John 11:17–19). And Jesus finally decided to pay a visit to His grieving friends. He told the disciples:

Our friend Lazarus has fallen asleep; but I go, so that I may awaken him out of sleep. (John 11:11)

GETTING TO THE ROOT

The Greek term *koimao* used in verse 11 literally means "asleep."[3] This word was used as a euphemism for death. However, the disciples misunderstood Jesus and believed that Lazarus was only sleeping, so Jesus had to tell them bluntly, "Lazarus is dead" (John 11:14).

When Martha heard that Jesus was coming, she ran out to meet Him on the road. She looked Him square in the eye and said, "Lord, if You had been here, my brother would not have died" (11:21). She felt betrayed by the only One who could have saved her brother's life.

Surely, we've felt the same way at times. We think to ourselves, "God, if only You had . . ." The tough stuff of death brings to the surface raw, unguarded emotions. Martha was angry—furious, outraged, mad! She couldn't believe Jesus had waited so long to arrive. She questioned His compassion and seemed to doubt His care and responsibility.

Could Jesus have prevented Lazarus's death? Absolutely. But He didn't. He deliberately chose to wait. Lazarus's death was part of God's sovereign plan—and that plan often contradicts our preferences. There's a divine mystery in the way He chooses to act because His ways are not our ways (Isaiah 55:8).

The day will come when God will allow death to have its way in your life and mine. Each of our loved ones will eventually pass away, too. For some, it will be before the end of this year. For others, it will be before the end of this decade. For many, it will seem terribly premature. For a few, it will come through a tragic accident. We know neither the time nor the manner in which we will breathe our last. Nevertheless, death will come for us all. That *is* a reality.

Some day in the future, when you and I least expect it, our number will be up. When that occurs, our families and friends may question God's goodness and His purposes, and they might wonder why God chose not to intervene and protect us. As it did during those dark days in Bethany, grief will sweep over our loved ones as they are forced to face exactly what Martha and Mary endured—the pain and finality of death.

But in the case of Lazarus, the story has an unusual twist.

A Miraculous Prayer

As Jesus approached the place where Lazarus had been buried, some of the people in the crowd began to accuse Jesus.

> Some of them said, "Could not this man, who opened the
> eyes of the blind man, have kept this man also from dying?"
> (John 11:37)

Doubt intensified in the minds of the grieving, especially because their faith rested on unsure footing. Experiencing a mixture of sadness and anger and grieved by the people's unbelief, Jesus authoritatively commanded, "Remove the stone" (11:39).

Remove the stone? Surely He couldn't be serious. Opening a closed grave was most unorthodox, not to mention the fact that it made a person ceremonially unclean according to the Mosaic Law. What did Jesus mean, "Remove the stone"? Martha protested loudly:

> Lord, by this time there will be a stench, for he has been dead four days. (John 11:39)

Note Jesus's response:

> "Did I not say to you that if you believe, you will see the glory of God?" So they removed the stone. Then Jesus raised His eyes, and said, "Father, I thank You that You have heard Me. I knew that You always hear Me; but because of the people standing around I said it, so that they may believe that You sent Me." When He had said these things, He cried out with a loud voice, "Lazarus, come forth." (John 11:40–43)

Jesus commanded the mourners to remove the stone that lay across Lazarus's grave. He then called loudly for Lazarus to arise and come out of the tomb.

From Fear to Faith

An eerie hush enveloped the crowd. Everyone stared at Jesus. What in the world was He thinking, calling for a dead man to come out of the tomb? Mary and Martha stood frozen in disbelief.

Suddenly, something moved within the shadowy darkness of the tomb. Impossible—or was it? Could it be? Yes, it was. Lazarus was alive!

> The man who had died came forth, bound hand and foot with wrappings, and his face was wrapped around with a cloth. Jesus said to them, "Unbind him, and let him go." (John 11:44)

New life sprang forth at the site of this humble grave as Jesus brought the breath of life back into Lazarus's decaying corpse. This incredible miracle illustrated Christ's grace, authority, and power as the Messiah.

TAKING TRUTH TO HEART

The death of a loved one causes even the most careless and carefree of souls to ponder eternal things. This was certainly the case with Lazarus's death. John tells us that "many of the Jews who came to Mary, and saw what He had done, believed in Him" (John 11:45). Jesus brought new life to those who were watching the events of Lazarus's death unfold—those who had been spiritually dead in their sin. What they witnessed changed their hearts and lives forever.

We're responsible to instill in others not only the reality of death, but also the hope of eternal life. Our life on earth provides only a fleeting prelude to the eternal life to come. We must live with the knowledge that every new day is a gift and a responsibility. We're called to share the hope of Christ with others before it's too late.

Why do you think Jesus waited until after Lazarus's death to arrive in Bethany? What effect did His choice have?

_____

_____

_____

_____

Raising a dead man was a much a greater miracle than healing a sick man. What do you think Mary, Martha, and the people of Bethany learned about Jesus through His raising of Lazarus? How do you think these lessons impacted their lives and the way they approached death in the future?

_____

_____

_____

_____

What principles from this passage can you apply personally when you face your own death or that of a loved one?

_____

_____

_____

_____

How can you offer hope to others facing the tough stuff of death?

_____

_____

_____

AND WHAT ABOUT YOU? WILL YOU BELIEVE?

Waiting before coming to Bethany enabled Jesus to fulfill two promises He made when He arrived. He gave the first promise to Martha when she met Him, sobbing, on the road. He said, "Your brother will rise again" (John 11:23). He promised Martha that she would see her brother alive again. Lazarus would not remain in the cold, dark tomb. He would experience the miracle of new life.

The second promise Jesus spoke to all who could hear. In fact, He continues to make it to all people everywhere. And what is that second promise? Jesus said,

> I am, right now, Resurrection and Life. The one who believes in me, even though he or she dies, will live. And everyone who lives believing in me does not ultimately die at all. *Do you believe this?* (John 11:25–26 MSG, emphasis added)

That is the fundamental question of life: *Do you believe this?* That's the question you will need to answer in the midst of your grief.

It turns out that the sentiment of the bumper sticker mentioned earlier—"Don't take life so seriously! You won't get out of it alive anyway"—was dead wrong. You *should* take life seriously, because spiritually, you *will* get out of it alive. Although your body may pass away, your spirit will live forever. So the question isn't, *Will you live forever?* but, *Where* will you live forever? In heaven with God, or in hell with Satan? It's your choice.

Jesus Christ alone holds the power of resurrection because He conquered the grave. The One who performed that unforgettable miracle on Lazarus later went to the cross and died, paying the complete penalty for your sin and mine. His loved ones wrapped His body in burial cloth, placed Him in a grave, and sealed His tomb with a stone. Three days later, He rose from the dead—freed from the grave and raised to life, never to die again. He conquered death and removed its sting forever.

Read John 11:25–26 again. How has Jesus demonstrated to you that He's the resurrection and the life? What does this phrase mean to you?

_____

_____

_____

_____

In what ways can you show others that your faith in Christ stands firm, even in the face of painful and difficult circumstances?

_____

_____

_____

_____

The apostle Paul believed in the awe-inspiring power of the resurrection:

> Neither death, nor life, nor angels, nor principalities, nor
> things present, nor things to come, nor powers, nor height,
> nor depth, nor any other created thing, will be able to sep-

arate us from the love of God, which is in Christ Jesus our Lord. (Romans 8:38–39)

Paul faced death without fear because of His relationship with Christ. That's why, toward the end of his courageous life, Paul could say with confidence, "For to me, to live is Christ and to die is gain" (Philippians 1:21).

Perhaps you just lost your mate of many years, a child to a tragic accident, or a close friend to some painful illness. Like no other, Jesus understands your despair. He's been there. He's endured the same pain and loneliness. If you're walking the painful path of watching a loved one die, cling to Jesus. Only a true, saving faith in Christ will take you and your family members beyond death to life. He alone holds the promise of resurrection and the hope of eternity. He is, right now, Resurrection and Life!

NOTES

Chapter 1 • Getting Through the Tough Stuff of Temptation
Unless otherwise noted below, all material in this chapter is based on or quoted from "Christ at the Crossroad of Temptation," a sermon by Charles R. Swindoll, March 4, 1990, and chapter 1 in the companion book, *Getting Through the Tough Stuff*. Portions of this chapter have been adapted from chapter 1 of the *Christ at the Crossroads* study guide.

1. Walter L. Liefeld, Donald A. Carson, Walter W. Wessell, and Frank E. Gaebelein, eds. *Expositor's Bible Commentary: The NT*, vol. 8. (Grand Rapids, MI: Zondervan, 1984). Used by permission of The Zondervan Corporation.

Chapter 2 • Getting Through the Tough Stuff of Misunderstanding
Unless otherwise noted below, all material in this chapter is based on or quoted from "Christ at the Crossroad of Misunderstanding," a sermon by Charles R. Swindoll, March 11, 1990, and chapter 2 in the companion book, *Getting Through the Tough Stuff*. Portions of this chapter have been adapted from chapter 2 of the *Christ at the Crossroads* study guide.

1. Ralph Waldo Emerson, *Emerson: Selections from Self-Reliance, Friendship, Compensation, and Other Great Writings*, comp. Stanley Hendricks (Kansas City, MO: Hallmark Cards, 1969), 41.

2. John Walvoord and Roy Zuck, eds. *The Bible Knowledge Commentary: New Testament,* (Colorado Springs: Victor Books, 1985), 115, 117. Used by permission of Cook Ministries. All rights reserved.

3. Grassmick, "Mark," in *The Bible Knowledge Commentary,* 117.

4. Walter W. Wessel, "Mark," in *The Expositor's Bible Commentary,* vol. 8, ed. Frank E. Gaebelein and J. D. Douglas (Grand Rapids, MI: Zondervan, 1984), 645.

Chapter 3 • Getting Through the Tough Stuff of Anxiety
Unless otherwise noted below, all material in this chapter is based on or quoted from "Christ at the Crossroad of Anxiety," a sermon by Charles R. Swindoll, March 18, 1990, and chapter 3 in the companion book, *Getting Through the Tough Stuff.* Portions of this chapter have been adapted from chapter 3 of the *Christ at the Crossroads* study guide.

1. David Wallechinsky, Irving Wallace, and Amy Wallace, *The Book of Lists* (New York: William Morrow, 1977), 469–470.

2. *Merriam-Webster's Collegiate Dictionary,* 10th ed., see "anxiety."

3. Ken Gire, Jr., *Intimate Moments with the Savior.* (Grand Rpids, MI: Zondervan 1989). Used by permission of The Zondervan Corporation.

4. Ken Gire, *The Reflective Life: Becoming More Spiritually Sensitive to the Everyday Moments of Life* (Colorado Springs: Chariot Victor Publishing, 1998), 113.

Chapter 4 • Getting Through the Tough Stuff of Shame
Unless otherwise noted below, all material in this chapter is based on or quoted from "Christ at the Crossroad of Shame," a sermon by Charles R. Swindoll, March 25, 1990, and chapter 4 in the companion book, *Getting Through the Tough Stuff.* Portions of this chapter have been adapted from chapter 4 of the *Christ at the Crossroads* study guide.

1. *Merriam-Webster's Collegiate Dictionary,* 10th ed., see "shame."

2. Robert L. Thomas, ed., *New American Standard Exhaustive Concordance of the Bible* (Nashville: Holman Bible Publishers, 1981), 1659.

3. William Barclay, *The Gospel of John*, vol. 2, rev. ed., The Daily Study Bible Series (Philadelphia: Westminster Press, 1975), 2.

4. Barclay, *The Gospel of John*, 3.

5. Peter Marshall, quoted in Catherine Marshall, *A Man Called Peter: The Story of Peter Marshall* (Grand Rapids, MI: Chosen Books, a division of Baker Publishing Group, 1951), 325. Used by permission.

Chapter 5 • Getting Through the Tough Stuff of Doubt

Unless otherwise noted below, all material in this chapter is based on or quoted from "Christ at the Crossroad of Doubt," a sermon by Charles R. Swindoll, April 22, 1990, and chapter 5 in the companion book, *Getting Through the Tough Stuff*. Portions of this chapter have been adapted from chapter 7 of the *Christ at the Crossroads* study guide.

1. Ewald M. Plass, comp., *What Luther Says: An Anthology*, vol. 1 (St. Louis: Concordia, 1959), 426.

2. Alfred Lord Tennyson, "In Memoriam," in *Masterpieces of Religious Verse*, ed. James Dalton Morrison (New York: Harper & Row, 1948), 387.

3. Robert L. Thomas, ed., *New American Standard Exhaustive Concordance of the Bible* (Nashville: Holman Bible Publishers, 1981), 1642.

4. *Issues and Answers in Jesus' Day*, Bible Study Guide (Fullerton, CA: Insight for Living, 1990), 2.

5. Daniel Taylor, *The Myth of Certainty* (Grand Rapids, MI: Zondervan Publishing House, 1992), 16. Used by permission.

Chapter 6 • Getting Through the Tough Stuff of Divorce

Unless otherwise noted below, all material in this chapter is based on or quoted from "Christ at the Crossroad of Divorce," a sermon by Charles R. Swindoll, May 27, 1990, and chapter 6 in the companion book, *Getting Through the Tough Stuff*. Portions of this chapter have been adapted from chapter 9 of the *Christ at the Crossroads* study guide.

1. Ed Young, *Romancing the Home: How to Have a Marriage That Sizzles* (Nashville: Broadman and Holman, 1994), 15. Used by permission of Ed Young.

2. Walter L. Liefelt, Donald A. Carson, Walter W. Wessell, and Frank E. Gaebelein, eds. *Expositor's Bible Commentary: The NT,* vol. 8. (Grand Rapids, MI: Zondervan, 1984). Used by permission of The Zondervan Corporation.

3. John R. W. Stott, *The Message of the Sermon on the Mount (Matthew 5–7),* rev. ed. of *Christian Counter-Culture,* The Bible Speaks Today series (Downers Grove, IL: InterVarsity Press, 1978), 95.

Chapter 7 • Getting Through the Tough Stuff of Remarriage
Unless otherwise noted below, all material in this chapter is based on or quoted from "Christ at the Crossroad of Remarriage," a sermon by Charles R. Swindoll, June 3, 1990, and chapter 7 in the companion book, *Getting Through the Tough Stuff.* Portions of this chapter have been adapted from chapter 10 of the *Christ at the Crossroads* study guide.

1. Robert L. Thomas, ed., *New American Standard Exhaustive Concordance of the Bible* (Nashville: Holman Bible Publishers, 1981), 1658.

2. Mike Mason, *The Mystery of Marriage* (Sisters, OR: Multnomah, 1985), 93. Used by permission.

Chapter 8 • Getting Through the Tough Stuff of Confrontation
Unless otherwise noted below, all material in this chapter is based on or quoted from "Christ at the Crossroad of Confrontation," a sermon by Charles R. Swindoll, May 20, 1990, and chapter 8 in the companion book, *Getting Through the Tough Stuff.* Portions of this chapter have been adapted from chapter 11 of the *Christ at the Crossroads* study guide.

1. Robert L. Thomas, ed., *New American Standard Exhaustive Concordance of the Bible* (Nashville: Holman Bible Publishers, 1981), 1589.

2. Thomas, ed., *New American Standard Exhaustive Concordance,* 1654.

Chapter 9 • Getting Through the Tough Stuff of Pain

Unless otherwise noted below, all material in this chapter is based on or quoted from "Christ at the Crossroad of Pain," a sermon by Charles R. Swindoll, June 10, 1990, and chapter 9 in the companion book, *Getting Through the Tough Stuff.* Portions of this chapter have been adapted from chapter 12 of the *Christ at the Crossroads* study guide.

1. Robert L. Thomas, ed., *New American Standard Exhaustive Concordance of the Bible* (Nashville: Holman Bible Publishers, 1981), 1548.
2. Philip D. Yancey, *Where Is God When It Hurts*—Hardcover. (Grand Rapids, MI: Zondervan, 1977, 1990). Used by permission of The Zondervan Corporation.

Chapter 10 • Getting Through the Tough Stuff of Prejudice

Unless otherwise noted below, all material in this chapter is based on or quoted from "Christ at the Crossroad of Prejudice," a sermon by Charles R. Swindoll, July 15, 1990, and chapter 10 in the companion book, *Getting Through the Tough Stuff.* Portions of this chapter have been adapted from chapter 13 of the *Christ at the Crossroads* study guide.

1. *Merriam-Webster's Collegiate Dictionary,* 10th ed., see "prejudice."
2. Robert L. Thomas, ed., *New American Standard Exhaustive Concordance of the Bible* (Nashville: Holman Bible Publishers, 1981), 1662.
3. Merrill F. Unger, *The New Unger's Bible Dictionary,* ed. R. K. Harrison (Chicago: Moody, 1988), see "Samaritans."

Chapter 11 • Getting Through the Tough Stuff of Hypocrisy

Unless otherwise noted below, all material in this chapter is based on or quoted from "Christ at the Crossroad of Hypocrisy," a sermon by Charles R. Swindoll, June 24, 1990, and chapter 11 in the companion book, *Getting Through the Tough Stuff.* Portions of this chapter have been adapted from chapter 14 of the *Christ at the Crossroads* study guide.

1. Thomas R. Ybarra, as quoted by Dr. Laurence J. Peter, *Peter's Quotations: Ideas for Our Time* (New York: Bantam Books, 1989), 84.

2. Robert L. Thomas, ed., *New American Standard Exhaustive Concordance of the Bible* (Nashville: Holman Bible Publishers, 1981), 1690.

3. *Merriam-Webster's Collegiate Dictionary*, 10th ed., see "hypocrisy."

4. William Barclay, *The Gospel of Matthew*, vol. 1, rev. ed., The Daily Study Bible Series (Philadelphia: Westminster Press, 1975), 235.

Chapter 12 • Getting Through the Tough Stuff of Inadequacy

Unless otherwise noted below, all material in this chapter is based on or quoted from "Christ at the Crossroad of Inadequacy," a sermon by Charles R. Swindoll, July 22, 1990, and chapter 12 in the companion book, *Getting Through the Tough Stuff*. Portions of this chapter have been adapted from chapter 17 of the *Christ at the Crossroads* study guide.

1. Robert L. Thomas, ed., *New American Standard Exhaustive Concordance of the Bible* (Nashville: Holman Bible Publishers, 1981), 1656.

2. Letter from a pastor's wife to Charles R. Swindoll, n.p., n.d.

Chapter 13 • Getting Through the Tough Stuff of Disqualification

Unless otherwise noted below, all material in this chapter is based on or quoted from "Christ at the Crossroad of Disqualification," a sermon by Charles R. Swindoll, July 8, 1990, and chapter 13 in the companion book, *Getting Through the Tough Stuff*. Portions of this chapter have been adapted from chapter 16 of the *Christ at the Crossroads* study guide.

1. Robert L. Thomas, ed., *New American Standard Exhaustive Concordance of the Bible* (Nashville: Holman Bible Publishers, 1981), 1628.

2. Henry Alford, *The Greek New Testament*, vol. 2, 6th ed. (New York: Lee, Shepard, and Dillingham, 1873), 551.

3. Thomas, ed., *New American Standard Exhaustive Concordance*, 1688.

4. Paul Harvey, "Sin's Peril." Available at http://www.thewayofpeace.org/sins_peril.html. Accessed on August 9, 2004.

Chapter 14 • Getting Through the Tough Stuff of Death
Unless otherwise noted below, all material in this chapter is based on or quoted from "Christ at the Crossroad of Death," a sermon by Charles R. Swindoll, April 15, 1990, and chapter 14 in the companion book, *Getting Through the Tough Stuff.* Portions of this chapter have been adapted from chapter 6 of the *Christ at the Crossroads* study guide.

1. Insight for Living would like to thank Mary Lou Bayly for permission to use an excerpt from her late husband, Joe Bayly's book, *The Last Thing We Talk About.* This work is currently published by Victor Books under the title *A Voice in the Wilderness: The Best of Joe Bayly.*
2. Woody Allen, quoted in Lloyd Cory, *Quote Unquote* (Wheaton, IL: Victor Books, 1977), 81.
3. Robert L. Thomas, ed., *New American Standard Exhaustive Concordance of the Bible* (Nashville: Broadman and Holman, 1981), 1661.

Books for Probing Further

We hope you've gained strength for your spiritual journey as you have traveled with us through the tough stuff of life. We pray that you've emerged from this study as a stronger, more faithful believer in Christ.

The following books will help you to keep pressing on despite life's challenges. We hope you'll choose several resources from the list to provide you with further encouragement and biblical principles to aid you in your spiritual walk.

Bayly, Joseph. *The Last Thing We Talk About: Help and Hope for Those Who Grieve.* Elgin, Ill.: Cook Communications Ministries International, updated edition, 1992.

Bodmer, Judy. *When Love Dies: How to Save a Hopeless Marriage.* Nashville: W Publishing Group, 1999.

Elliot, Elisabeth. *A Path Through Suffering: Discovering the Relationship Between God's Mercy and Our Pain.* Ann Arbor, Mich.: Vine Books, 1992.

Ethridge, Shannon. *Every Woman's Battle: Discovering God's Plan for Sexual and Emotional Fulfillment.* Colorado Springs: WaterBrook Press, 2003.

Gire, Ken. *The Weathering Grace of God: The Beauty God Brings from Life's Upheavals.* Ann Arbor, Mich.: Vine Books, 2001.

Lewis, C. S. *The Problem of Pain.* San Francisco: HarperSanFrancisco, 2001.

Smedes, Lewis B. *Shame and Grace: Healing the Shame We Don't Deserve,* reprinted. San Francisco: HarperSanFrancisco, 1994.

Weaver, Joanna. *Having a Mary Heart in a Martha World: Finding Intimacy with God in the Busyness of Life.* Colorado Springs: WaterBrook Press, 2000.

Wheat, Ed. *How to Save Your Marriage Alone.* Grand Rapids, Mich.: Zondervan Publishing Company, 1983.

Wilson, Sandra D. *Released from Shame: Moving Beyond the Pain of the Past,* rev. ed. Downers Grove, Ill.: InterVarsity Press, 2002.

Yancey, Philip. *Disappointment with God: Three Questions No One Asks Aloud.* Grand Rapids, Mich.: Zondervan Publishing Company, 1997.